Lecture Notes in Computer Science   662

Edited by G. Goos and J. Hartmanis

Advisory Board: W. Brauer   D. Gries   J. Stoer

M. Nitzberg   D. Mumford   T. Shiota

Filtering, Segmentation and Depth

Springer-Verlag

Berlin Heidelberg New York
London Paris Tokyo
Hong Kong Barcelona
Budapest

Series Editors

Gerhard Goos
Universität Karlsruhe
Postfach 69 80
Vincenz-Priessnitz-Straße 1
W-7500 Karlsruhe, FRG

Juris Hartmanis
Cornell University
Department of Computer Science
4130 Upson Hall
Ithaca, NY 14853, USA

Authors

Mark Nitzberg
David Mumford
Department of Mathematics, Harvard University
Cambridge, MA 02183, USA

Takahiro Shiota
Department of Mathematics, Kyoto University
Kyoto, Japan

CR Subject Classification (1991): I.4.3, I.4.6, I.4.8, I.4.10, I.2.10

ISBN 3-540-56484-5 Springer-Verlag Berlin Heidelberg New York
ISBN 0-387-56484-5 Springer-Verlag New York Berlin Heidelberg

© Springer-Verlag Berlin Heidelberg 1993
Printed in Germany

Typesetting: Camera ready by author/editor
45/3140-543210 - Printed on acid-free paper

Preface

Computer vision seeks a process that starts with a noisy, ambiguous signal from a TV camera and ends with a high-level description of discrete objects located in 3-dimensional space and identified in a human classification. In this book we address this process at several levels. We first treat the low-level image-processing issues of noise removal and smoothing while preserving important lines and singularities in an image. At a slightly higher level, we describe a robust contour tracing algorithm that produces a cartoon of the important lines in the image. Finally, we begin the high-level task of reconstructing the geometry of objects in the scene.

The problems in computer vision are so interrelated that to solve one we must solve them all. This book manages to make serious progress at several levels of visual reconstruction by working in a restricted world of simple pictures of simple objects.

We use a model that represents a scene as a group of overlapping shapes corresponding to the projections of objects. In constructing this representation from an image, the algorithm must imitate the process in human perception of inferring contours and surfaces that are occluded or are not present in the luminance function. Consequently, the work depends strongly on what we know about the psychology of perception, especially from the Gestalt school and its heirs.

We define the problem in this way: to find a decomposition of the domain D of an image that has the fewest disrupted edges–junctions of edges, crack tips, corners, and cusps–by creating suitable continuations for the disrupted edges. The result is a decomposition of D into overlapping regions $R_1 \cup ... \cup R_n$ ordered by occlusion, called the 2.1-D Sketch.

Chapters 2 through 5 describe algorithms that have been implemented in the C language for a SUN workstation running Unix[1] and X-Windows, using a library of computer vision functions called HVision. The programs from this book are available via anonymous FTP from internet host math.harvard.edu, in the directory vision.

If computer vision is to have a hope of serious long-term progress in the engineering sense, we must adopt the tradition from the numerical analysis community of sharing computer code. In this way, the next generation of results is built upon the combined best parts of the previous generation.

---

[1]Unix is a trademark of AT&T Bell Laboratories

vi

The authors gratefully acknowledge the support of the National Science and Technology Research Center for Computation and Visualization of Geometric Structures.

October 1992   Mark Nitzberg
                                                                    David Mumford
                                                                    Takahiro Shiota

(Left to right: David Mumford, Takahiro Shiota, Mark Nitzberg)

Contents

Figure 0.1: Still life with subliminal ad for local grocery store

Chapter 1

Overview

In the picture on the facing page, the potato partly covers the nectarine and also hides part of the bottle. This partial overlap, or *occlusion*, of farther objects by those nearer, is one of the most fundamental obstacles that the visual system must overcome to achieve its goal of recognizing and locating objects in our three-dimensional world.

Most of the structurally important lines in what we see are the boundaries that separate objects from the view of the things behind them. For the past 25 years, researchers in computer vision have been trying to find lines and edges in images in order to recognize objects automatically. What has been missing in this endeavor is that most of what we see is partially covered by something nearer. In this book we have tried to lay out a practical way of incorporating occlusion into the task of finding object outlines.

Can we really believe that occlusion is detected at a low level? Even without stereopsis and motion cues, we can experience a striking impression of depth from a single, stationary retinal image such as from a photograph or painting. The main cue to occlusion in this setting comes from the points where objects overlap in a scene. These are *edge terminations*, which occur most often where one object outline stops, abruptly abuts against the outline of a nearer object, and forms a junction in the shape of the capital letter 'T'. Look again at the still life, and note how nearly all the occlusion relations can be readily computed based on the T-junctions.

One theory has it that the impression that one fruit is in front of another comes from first recognizing the objects, or at least familiar shapes, and then noticing that they are incomplete examples of those shapes. This implies that we have already performed a difficult task–to recognize a shape from an incomplete example of it–in order then to infer that it is indeed incomplete, and therefore partly occluded. A more plausible model for early visual organization, and one which psychologists support increasingly, is a process driven by locating disrupted boundaries and building continuations for them behind occluding surfaces, with recognition coming later. By reconstructing just this first "bit" of the third dimension, the visual system has simpler shape data from which to find objects.

Here are two illustrations of how higher-level cognition does not have a decisive effect on visual organization. Firstly, we readily perceive occlusion among unfamiliar shapes, as in Figure 1.1. This supports the idea that familiar shape is not necessarily what tells us which vegetable is in front of which in the still life. Secondly, the contemporary psychologist Gaetano Kanizsa, notable as much for his art as for his psychology, has

Figure 1.1: One unfamiliar shape occludes another.

sketched pictures for which our perception directly contradicts what we know about the world. In figure 1.2, for example, the man and woman are entangled in the fence. Knowing that they are behind the fence does not change this unusual perception. Thus perceptual organization follows its own set of rules that depend decisively on occlusion but not on higher-level object recognition. Simply put, we navigate in the world successfully by seeing what's in front of what independently of knowing what's what.

In this book we make explicit some of the these hidden rules of perceptual organization, and then cast them in a model that lets us compute the relative depth of objects from occlusion cues–in other words, to find depth from overlap.

1.1   Segmenting with depth

We propose a model that lets us reconstruct object shapes from a picture of several interposed objects, including parts that are occluded by nearer objects. The model also determines the nearness relations of the objects.

This is a novel approach to one of the principal goals of computer vision, that of *segmenting* an image. Roughly speaking, to segment means to find regions of interest in a picture, so that these regions can be parceled out for further analysis. The ultimate aim of our algorithm will be similar; however, regions of interest will now be allowed to overlap and occlude one another, and in addition, the hidden parts of incomplete regions will be restored by hypothetical completions.

Image segmentation has come to mean the process of cutting up a picture into the simplest shaped pieces possible while keeping the color or luminance of each piece as uniform as possible. An image is given as a function $g(x, y), (x, y) \epsilon D$ representing the light intensity or color vector produced by a 3D world and striking a lens from direction (x, y). The aim is to segment the domain D, i.e. partition D into regions $R_1, \ldots, R_k$ such that R_i is the part of the image in which the nearest object is some object O_i and on the boundary between any two regions R_i and R_j, object O_i occludes object O_j or vice-versa.

This assumes that we have some decisive way to find the regions that correspond to distinct objects. In general, the variety of lighting situations, surface characteristics and textures in the world make it necessary to integrate visual input of various types: depth cues from stereo and motion, texture boundaries, shading and shadows. To build a practical system, we restrict ourselves to single, stationary images of objects with uniform nontextured surfaces where shadows and shading do not hide important object features.

Figure 1.2: The man and woman are entangled in the fence.

Our model also addresses another goal of vision, that of computing or estimating what David Marr called the $2\frac{1}{2}$D sketch associated to an image [24]; i.e., the depth image $z(x, y)$ recording the distance from the lens to the nearest object in the direction (x, y) and its normalized partial derivatives:

$$p(x,y) = z_x/\sqrt{1 + z_x^2 + z_y^2}$$
$$q(x,y) = z_y/\sqrt{1 + z_x^2 + z_y^2}$$

Marr proposed multiple sources of information contained in the intensity image $g(x, y)$ from which one could hope to estimate the $2\frac{1}{2}$D sketch (z, p, q). This too has proved hard to implement except under strong constraints, for example, where very accurate stereo or motion data is available, or where the lighting and surface reflectances are heavily constrained.

Our model achieves a synthesis of these two goals, segmentation and the $2\frac{1}{2}$D sketch, while avoiding the numerical burden of the $2\frac{1}{2}$D sketch and at the same time simplifying 2D segmentation by incorporating occlusion explicitly. Hence in the language of computer vision, we might call our model the 2.1D sketch.

Consider figure 1.3(a), an image of several blades of grass against a light background. Figure 1.3(b) shows the 12 disjoint regions that result from cutting (a) along visible object boundaries. However, the 12 regions do not correspond to 12 distinct objects in the world: there are only 4 objects reflecting light—the 3 blades of grass and the background "object". Although each of the original objects lies at varying depth, there is a simple ordering of the objects that indicates which objects occlude which. We can describe the scene as a stage set with 4 "wings", transparent except where they contain an object. The background is last in the set and is everywhere opaque. This is shown in figure 1.3(c).

This is what we mean by a 2.1D sketch: it is a set of regions R_i in the domain D of the image which fill up D but which may overlap, plus a partial ordering $<$ on the regions indicating which are in front of which others. Often there will be a background object R_0 behind all others for which $R_0 = D$. Our contention is that this type of segmentation is more natural than the kind with disjoint, unordered R_i and that it captures the most accessible part of the $2\frac{1}{2}$D sketch.

1.2   Edge terminations and continuations

The chief reason we expect the 2.1D sketch to be readily computable is the presence of edge terminations, and in particular T-junctions. T-junctions are points where the edges in the image form a "T", with one edge Γ_1 ending abruptly in the middle of a second edge Γ_2. Such points often arise because Γ_2 is an occlusion edge and Γ_1 is any kind of edge—occlusion, shadow, surface-marking—of a more distant object whose continuation disappears behind Γ_2.

The importance of T-junctions in the human visual system has been known for a long time, but their role and power have been greatly clarified by recent work. In particular, it has become increasingly clear that T-junctions are computed early in the visual process and are not merely part of an object recognition paradigm as in the early blocks world algorithms of Guzman, Roberts, Waltz, etc (cf. [39]). The gestalt school of psychology and, particularly, the contemporary psychologist Gaetano Kanizsa have made a thorough and deep analysis of T-junctions [17]. Consider figure 1.4 from Kanizsa. 1.4(a) and 1.4(b) differ only in the addition of diagonal lines which change the corners in 1.4(a) to T-junctions in 1.4(b); 1.4(b) is unmistakably 3-dimensional. More importantly, we infer that something is being occluded and fill in the hidden parts. 1.4(a) and 1.4(c) differ only in the subtraction of short connecting lines which change corners in 1.4(a) to terminators in 1.4(c).

A terminating line is a weak form of T-junction in that it signals occlusion approximately perpendicular to the line at its end. Likewise corners can be thought of as degenerate forms of T-junctions, especially when pairs of their edges are aligned, as in Kanizsa's triangle illusion (see figure 1.5). In general, when several edge terminations are aligned, we tend to perceive a contour "connecting" the terminations along which one surface occludes another. The alignment of terminations seems to cause the hypothetical T-junctions to mutually confirm one another.

A striking confirmation of the reality of these so-called illusions and the illusory contours that we see was found by R. von der Heydt and his colleagues [15]. The responses of single cells in visual areas are codified by describing their visual field: the area within which moving or stationary bars and edges produce activity. They found, however, that many cells in visual area V2[1] responded when no actual stimulus was

---

[1]Known as Brodmann area 18 in man, this area is adjacent to the primary visual area V1 (= area 17 = striate cortex) and is a recipient of a high proportion of its axonal output.

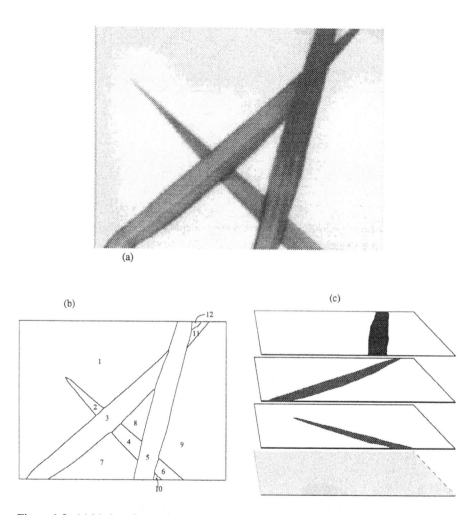

Figure 1.3: (a) blades of grass image; (b) a disjoint segmentation; (c) a segmentation with overlaps.

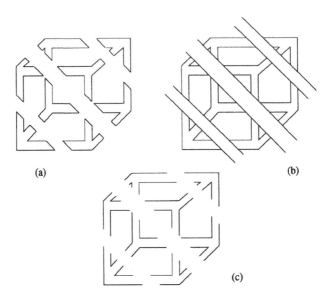

Figure 1.4: A demonstration from Kanizsa of the importance of T-junctions and terminators.

Figure 1.5: Kanizsa's triangle illusion: not three Pac-Man shapes, but three circles occluded by a nearer white triangle.

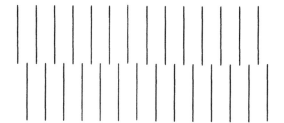

Figure 1.6: Aligned terminators elicit neuronal responses along the subjective contour.

present in their visual field, but rather when edges outside this field produced illusory contours that crossed the field. Thus, stimuli such as in figure 1.6 evoke responses from "horizontal line-detector" cells whose job is normally to find horizontal lines of high contrast.

In all these cases, the mind seems to create a 3D scene in which occluded parts of visible objects are reconstructed. In the case of the Kanizsa triangle, the mind goes further and creates missing outlines of the nearer occluding triangle, and compensates for their absence in the raw data by a perceptual impression that the white triangle is brighter than the more distant white background.

Contours such as as the sides of the Kanizsa triangle are known as subjective contours, because they are not present in the gray level image, yet they are particularly vivid under certain circumstances. Nakayama and Shimojo [31] have studied the mechanics of these subjective surfaces, and have produced numerous demonstrations that the pictorial cues to occlusion are used in an early processing stage of human vision that drives the grouping processes. Theirs and related results in psychology that bear directly on the 2.1D sketch model are discussed in Chapter 4.

1.3 A variational model

To set down the requirements of the 2.1D sketch more precisely, we define an energy functional that takes its minimum at an optimal 2.1D sketch of an input image. We begin by recalling the variational model used for image segmentation without overlaps.

The piecewise smooth model of the segmentation problem in computer vision asks how to clip a picture into as few and simple pieces as possible while keeping the color of each piece as smooth and/or slowly varying as possible. One approach to the problem, taken by Mumford and Shah [28], is to define a functional that takes its minimum at an optimal piecewise smooth approximation to a given image. The image is a function g defined on a domain D in the plane. It is approximated by a function f, which is smooth except at a finite set Γ of piecewise C^1 contours which meet ∂D and meet each other only at their endpoints. The functional defined below gives a measure of the match between an image g and a segmentation f, Γ:

$$E_{\text{M-S}}(f, \Gamma) = \mu^2 \int_D (f - g)^2 d\mathbf{x} + \int_{D \backslash \Gamma} \|\nabla f\|^2 d\mathbf{x} + \nu \int_\Gamma ds.$$

The first term asks that f approximate g, the second asks that f vary slowly except at boundaries, and the third asks that the set of contours be as short, and hence as simple and straight as possible. The contours of Γ cut D into a finite set of disjoint regions $R_1, \ldots, R_n$, the connected components of $D \backslash \Gamma$.

In this book, however, we seek a model that incorporates partially the way that g derives from a 2D projection of a 3D scene. Rather than base our 2.1D model on a set of curves Γ that cuts D into disjoint regions, we ask for a set of regions R_i whose union equals D, and with a partial ordering that represents relative depth. The overlapping of regions gives in a sense the most primitive depth information. The domain D is considered as a window that reveals the value of g only on a portion of the plane. As a result, contour integrals will exclude portions of a contour that coincide with the boundary of D.

We now seek a functional $E_{2.1}$ much like $E_{\text{M-S}}$ that achieves a minimum at the optimal overlapping segmentation of g. Let $\{R_1, \ldots, R_n\}$ be a set of regions such that $\bigcup_i R_i = D$, with a partial ordering $<$ that represents occlusion, e.g., $R_i < R_j$ means R_i occludes R_j.

$$R_i' = R_i \backslash \bigcup_{R_i < R_j} R_j$$

is the "visible" portion of R_i. Throughout the book, R_i denotes a closed subset of D with piecewise smooth boundary and connected interior. The expression $(\{R_i\}, <)$ denotes an ordered set of overlapping regions, which we will call a *segmentation*.

We then define the energy $E_{2.1}(\{R_i\}, <)$ as

$$\sum_{i=1}^{n} \left(\mu^2 \int_{R_i'} (g - m_i)^2 d\mathbf{x} + \epsilon \int_{R_i} d\mathbf{x} + \int_{\partial R_i \backslash \partial D} \phi(\kappa) ds \right).$$

In this formula, m_i is the mean of g on R_i', and κ is the curvature of ∂R_i, i.e. $\|\ddot{\gamma}\|$ where γ parameterizes ∂R_i by arc length. The function $\phi : \mathbf{R} \to \mathbf{R}$ is defined by

$$\phi(\kappa) = \begin{cases} \nu + \alpha \kappa^2 & \text{for } |\kappa| < \beta/\alpha \\ \nu + \beta|\kappa| & \text{for } |\kappa| \geq \beta/\alpha \end{cases}.$$

The scalar constants μ, ν, ϵ, α and β in the definition of ϕ, determine the characteristics of a segmentation which minimizes $E_{2.1}$. Their dimensions are:

$$
\begin{aligned}
\mu &\sim \text{intensity}^{-1}.\text{dist.}^{-1} \\
\nu &\sim \text{dist.}^{-1} \\
\alpha &\sim \text{dist.} \\
\beta &\sim \text{dimensionless} \\
\epsilon &\sim \text{dist.}^{-2}
\end{aligned}
$$

Before analyzing the functional, we should describe its relation to the 2.1D sketch *model*, and to the computer algorithm that finds the 2.1D sketch of an image. The model refers to the representation of an image by a set of possibly overlapping shapes, together with depth relations between them. Writing down a functional $E_{2.1}$ is a way of describing concisely what makes a good set of shapes for a given image. For example, the first term of $E_{2.1}$ asks that the various visible parts of a single region ought to be of nearly the same brightness, and the third term asks that contours be short and wiggle as little as possible. The functional also asks to minimize the number of corners even if by introducing new contours; these are the continuations of partly occluded contours. Minimizing $E_{2.1}$ as defined, however, would make sense only in a world with surfaces of constant color.

Our algorithm does not minimize the functional as such. It first segments the image along lines of high contrast, then adds continuations using part of the definition of $E_{2.1}$, and finally finds the optimal 2.1D sketch by explicitly minimizing $E_{2.1}$ over the finite number of ways of assembling these contours into boundaries of regions. The edge-finding process can be improved arbitrarily as we discover better ways to find object boundaries.

Input images.

Our model can represent simple pictures of interposed objects that are not woven nor self-overlapping, and whose object boundaries correspond almost exactly to long lines of high contrast (either light/dark boundaries or dark or bright lines).

Initial edges, with no continuations, come from an algorithm based loosely on Canny's line-finding algorithm [5]. Consequently the 2.1D sketch algorithm will succeed on images for which this initial edge detector yields the outlines of objects in the scene exactly, possibly with a few other edges. Shadows and texture must be minimal so they do not obscure important segments of an edge, and specular highlights cannot meet other object boundaries.

Moreover, edges must be occlusion edges rather than abrupt changes in surface normal direction. The algorithm has as yet no equipment to interpret 3D geometry from the edges along creases, such as where two walls meet, and such as we see every day in our world of geometric architecture and furniture. In addition, the kind of T-junction that comes from a shirt sleeve running behind an arm deserves special attention. Figure 1.7 shows two kinds of junctions a and b. The first is the prototypical T-junction where one object outline disappears behind a nearer object. The second is a single object with a surface marking that "disappears" from view at the object boundary. This is the case with surface markings, some shadows, and thin coverings such as a shirt sleeve. From almost all angles, the projected junction b is a cusp. Thus by discriminating between ordinary T-junctions and cusps, one could avoid erroneous figure-ground interpretations.

Unfortunately, our digital pictures do not have enough resolution to determine precisely the angles at T-junctions. The algorithm must allow several interpretations of each T-junction, since it cannot distinguish these two types. It then eliminates impossible choices in what is commonly called a "relaxation labeling" process [44]. This is discussed in Chapter 4.

Properties of $E_{2.1}$.

The first and second terms of $E_{2.1}$ are easily seen to give, on R'_i:

$$(\text{variance}_{R'_i}(g) + \epsilon) \cdot \text{area}(R'_i).$$

This is the basic term that keeps g close to constant on each region; without it, the trivial segmentation ($\{D\}$) achieves a minimum of E.

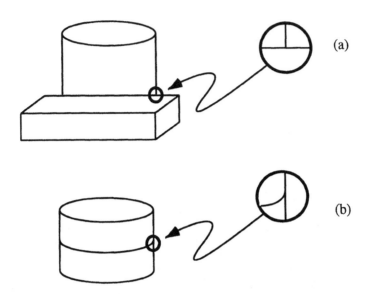

Figure 1.7: Local differences between two common sources of T-junctions. (a) the edge
of one object disappears behind a nearer object, forming a T or skewed T; (b) a surface-
marking stops where the surface falls out of view, forming a cusp from almost all points
of view.

The second term of $E_{2.1}$ gives a penalty for the total area of all regions. Its purpose is
to encourage segmentations in which small regions occlude larger ones. Without an area
term, the segmentations shown for figure 1.8(a), in figures 1.8(b) and (c) give the same
value for E; with an area term (c) gives a lower value for E. Moreover, without an area
term, the functional would not penalize any number of regions completely hidden behind
the rearmost background region. The parameter ϵ should be very small, because the area
term is intended to create distinctions in otherwise ambiguous situations.

The third term asks that the boundaries of regions in the interior of D be short and
not too curvy. It equals ν times the length of $\partial R_i - \partial D$ plus α times the integral of
the curvature squared along the same boundary, except where curvature exceeds β/α,
whereupon the term becomes β times the integral of the curvature. Note that the integral
of the curvature over a piece γ of ∂R_i is just the total angle through which γ turns. This
term discourages region boundaries from tracing circuitous level-curves in their effort
to minimize the variance term. Moreover, this term determines a family of contours
that comprises the ideal continuations of disrupted edges behind occluding regions. The
psychology and computation of these contours is the subject of Chapter 3.

The purpose of $\phi(\cdot)$ changing from a quadratic to a linear function at β/α is to allow
us to extend the definition of the second term to a contour which is smooth except at a
finite number of infinite-curvature points, or "corners." (Intervals of very high curvature
are also treated like corners in this formulation.) Suppose a contour γ parameterized
by arc-length has corner points and intervals $c_1, \ldots, c_k$ along which curvature $> \beta/\alpha$,
$C = \cup_i c_i \subset [0, 1]$. Let arg $\dot{\gamma}$ denote the angle between the tangent to γ and the positive

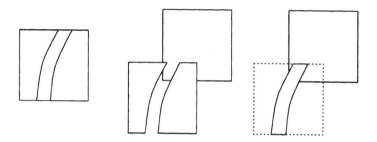

Figure 1.8: A simple image with two edges and two possible 2.1D Sketches.

x-axis. Then the curvature term for γ is given by

$$\alpha \int_{\gamma \backslash C} \ddot{\gamma}^2 ds + \beta \sum_{c \in C} |\arg \dot{\gamma}\,(c_+) - \arg \dot{\gamma}\,(c_-)|,$$

where c_- and c_+ are the left and right hand sides of interval c. In other words, the penalty for a corner point or interval of high curvature is proportional to the change in tangent direction at the corner or over the interval.

1.4 A computer algorithm

The most concrete product from this research is a segmentation algorithm that finds the 2.1D sketch of an intensity image I. The book is organized in sections that describe the stages of the algorithm. Again, this book does not attempt to solve the variational problem of minimizing $E_{2.1}$ in general. Even the simpler case of minimizing the third term does not have a closed-form solution expressible in elementary functions.

The algorithm finds the 2.1D sketch of an image in three stages: finding edges and junctions, building plausible continuations of disrupted edges, and minimizing $E_{2.1}$ combinatorially with these edges and continuations.

The first stage of the algorithm finds thin dark or bright lines and lines of high contrast; edges are traced using a hysteresis similar to that used by Canny [5]. However, since the crucial cues to occlusion are corners and T-junctions, a simple Gaussian blurring is inappropriate for preprocessing. We instead apply a nonlinear filter that localizes edges while preserving corners and T-junctions. Chapter 2 describes this nonlinear filter in detail. A pseudo-code implementation is given in Appendix B.

Chapter 3 details the edge-tracing algorithm. The algorithm assembles edge points into curves, using the detected orientation as as an initial estimate of edge tangent. This gives a set of curves $\Gamma = \{\gamma_1, \cdots, \gamma_k\}$ which do not intersect. Their endpoints are joined to nearby curves both to jump small gaps in edges and to form T-junctions and corners. The position, tangent angle, and curvature is refined at each point along the assembled curves by computing a best-fit to a circle or line on some fixed number of points along the edge. Endpoints $\gamma_i(0)$ and $\gamma_i(1)$, are tagged as corners where a cornerness measure is above some threshold; triple points are marked as well. For each gap filled by joining two loose endpoints, we delete the two fragments of curves from Γ and add the completed curve to Γ. At T-junctions and corners, we split the curves, so that now $\Gamma = \{\gamma_1, \ldots, \gamma_h\}$ is a set of curves which meet each other only at their endpoints. Contour-detection and curve-smoothing algorithms are given in pseudo-code in Appendix B.

Chapter 4 treats the problem of computing continuations of disrupted contours. The work of psychologists G. Kanizsa, K. Nakayama, and others has yielded a better understanding of the mechanics of continuations in human vision. The chapter begins by reviewing principles that one might conjecture from the psychology. It goes on to explain our approach to building continuations in relation to these principles.

To build continuations the algorithm computes new contours from edge terminations by matching up pairs of endpoints, disqualifying unlikely matches via several heuristics, and computing continuations for the remaining candidate pairs. Continuation curves are computed to approximate minima of a sum of length and the square of curvature with the given endpoints and end tangents. The algorithm uses a cubic spline which minimizes this term, rather than the general minimizing curve, to save hours of computer time. We also propose the idea of using a table of more or less likely continuations precomputed from a stochastic process; this is not yet incorporated into the program.

To disqualify most pairs of endpoints, one heuristic requires the length scale of a continuation to be of a reasonably close proportion to the lengths of the curve segments being joined. Thus if two curves of length 1 are 5 units apart, they are disqualified. Another heuristic requires that matching T-junctions have similar intensity on at least one side of the base of the T, or if not, that the light/dark relation at one T match up with the other. A third heuristic disqualifies a continuation if it forces an impossible ordering of regions based on the interpretations of the T-junctions.

The new curves $\{\gamma_{h+1}, \ldots, \gamma_g\}$ are added to Γ, and are marked as "continuations." When a new contour intersects others, they are both split at the intersection to keep the γ_i meeting only at endpoints.

The parameters ν and α in the $E_{2.1}$ are used in building the continuations, and dictate which set of continuations is best. The algorithm can find several different 2.1D sketches for a single picture, all of which are plausible interpretations of the objects in the scene.

Chapter 5 describes the third and final stage of the algorithm, which minimizes $E_{2.1}$ on I by combinatoric search to find the optimal segmentation wherein all region boundaries lie along contours in Γ. This search is made somewhat more efficient by working effectively from front to back, from smaller to larger sets of regions, and by using a Γ with only one set of consistent continuation edges added. However, the algorithm is exponential, so that it is practical only on simple images. Results are analyzed with a number of images for which the system yields the perceptually correct result, and on images that yield wrong interpretations.

Finally, Chapter 6 reviews the major obstacles tackled by the algorithm, and discusses areas of potential improvement.

Chapter 2

Filtering for Occlusion Detection

This chapter describes a blurring/sharpening algorithm that enhances strong edges and eliminates noise and weak edges, while preserving corners and T-junctions.

The algorithm follows naturally from methods of adaptive smoothing first used for noise cleaning in television pictures by Graham in the late 1950s [13], and subsequently rediscovered by several others [33, 20, 29]. These methods use a local edge-ness estimate to determine a variable weighting function for averaging. Each point is replaced by an average of nearby intensities which are located *away* from a nearby edge. It is useful to look closely at Graham's algorithm for background.

Graham was among the first to use equipment for digital computer processing of pictures. His algorithm was based on the idea that noise is less obvious to the eye, and therefore less of a problem, in the regions of an image with more detail. Anyone who plays the piano knows the analogous fact that a mistake made playing a simple piece like a Mozart sonata is disasterously obvious, while a mistake made playing the florid part of a Liszt rhapsody is unnoticeable. Graham therefore devised a method that blurs more in uniform regions of the picture than in busy parts. He used a second difference computed on nearest neighbors as a local measure of the level of detail.

Let $I(\mathbf{x}) \in \mathbf{R}$ be a sampled input image, that is, with $\mathbf{x} \in D = \{1 \ldots \text{width}\} \times \{1 \ldots \text{height}\}$. Graham's method approximates the second partials I_{xx} and I_{yy} of the image I by the discrete convolutions with the 3×3 kernels:

$$\begin{pmatrix} 1/6 & -1/3 & 1/6 \\ 1/6 & -1/3 & 1/6 \\ 1/6 & -1/3 & 1/6 \end{pmatrix} \text{ and } \begin{pmatrix} 1/6 & 1/6 & 1/6 \\ -1/3 & -1/3 & -1/3 \\ 1/6 & 1/6 & 1/6 \end{pmatrix}$$

respectively. Then at each pixel p, one replaces p by a weighted average of $I(p)$ and zero or more of its neighbors, depending on whether the values $I_{xx}(p)$ and $I_{yy}(p)$ fall below or above a threshold δ, which is typically two percent of the range of I. Labelling p's eight grid neighbors with compass directions, the algorithm replaces each $I(p)$ by

$$\begin{aligned} (p + \text{all neighbors})/9 \quad & \text{if } I_{xx} < \delta \text{ and } I_{yy} < \delta \\ (p + E + W)/3 \quad & \text{if } I_{xx} < \delta \text{ and } I_{yy} \geq \delta \\ (p + N + S)/3 \quad & \text{if } I_{xx} \geq \delta \text{ and } I_{yy} < \delta, \text{ and} \\ p \text{ itself} \quad & \text{if } I_{xx} \geq \delta \text{ and } I_{yy} \geq \delta, \end{aligned}$$

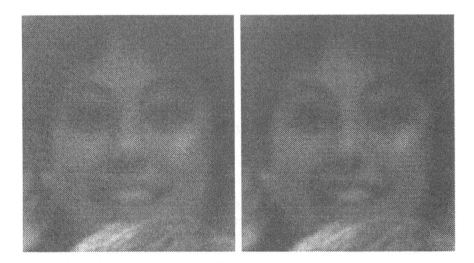

Figure 2.1: Left: a blurred, noisy image of a face (courtesy of E. Migliorini). Right: after applying Graham's noise-cleaning algorithm

where p, E, W, N, and S are used to denote the image intensities $I(p)$, etc. at those points. In plain English, if the picture wiggles in the x direction, blur in the y direction, if it doesn't wiggle, blur in both directions, and so on. Results are shown in figure 2.1. Graham's algorithm leaves the very dark noise pixels with $0.1\% \leq \delta \leq 0.5\%$. Within this range, the algorithm blurs about a quarter of the pixels in the x direction only, a quarter in the y direction only, and a quarter in both directions; the last quarter are not blurred. A lower threshold yields uniform smoothing in all directions; a higher threshold gives almost no smoothing at all. In any case, the algorithm does not sharpen salient edges, and it does round corners.

Our filter is a continuous form that generalizes this idea of blurring along but not across edges; points in a neighborhood away from a nearby edge are given stronger weight. Graham's use of second derivatives is approximated by our filter's integration of directional first derivatives (refer to section 2.3).

We define an image in the usual way as an intensity function $I(\mathbf{x})$ defined on a domain $D \subset \mathbf{R}^2$, and we use *edge* somewhat loosely to mean the boundary between two regions of relatively uniform intensity in an image, indicated by a strong gradient of I.

The filter algorithm computes a new image I_{out} by applying, at each point $\mathbf{x}_0$, a variable Gaussian kernel that is shaped, scaled and displaced according to the gradient of I in a neighborhood of $\mathbf{x}_0$:

$$I_{\text{out}}(\mathbf{x}_0) = \frac{1}{Z(\mathbf{x}_0)} \int_D k(\mathbf{x}_0, \mathbf{x}) I(\mathbf{x}) d\mathbf{x} \qquad (2.1)$$

where $Z(\mathbf{x}_0) = \int_D k(\mathbf{x}_0, \mathbf{x}) d\mathbf{x}$ is a normalizing factor. Normalization guarantees the maximum principle, so that $\max_D I_{\text{out}} \leq \max_D I$, and $\min_D I_{\text{out}} \geq \min_D I$.

In our implementation the boundary of the image is treated with a Neumann type boundary condition. The image is extended to a large enough neighborhood D' of D by reflection at the boundary, so that in equation (2.1) the integral can be performed over D' for all x_0 in D without changing the formulas.

The kernel for the point x_0 is defined by

$$\frac{1}{Z(x_0)}k(x_0, x) = \frac{1}{Z(x_0)}\rho_1(x - x_0 + \alpha(x_0))e^{-Q_{x_0}(x-x_0+\alpha(x_0))}, \qquad (2.1')$$

where Q_{x_0} is a quadratic form, and α is a vector that gives the negative of the displacement of the kernel from x_0. In coordinates (x, y) with the origin at $x_0 - \alpha(x_0)$, the kernel can be written

$$\frac{1}{Z(x_0)}\rho_1(x, y)e^{-(Ex^2+2Fxy+Gy^2)/\sigma^2},$$

with E, F and G values computed once for each x_0, as shown below. ρ_1 is a cut-off function centered at the origin that limits the effective size of the kernel, and σ is a parameter that scales the Gaussian bump. The diameter of the effective support of ρ_1 is called the *kernel size*. We assume that the cut-off function ρ_1 here, as well as ρ_2 and ρ_3 mentioned below, are rotationally symmetric, and are normalized to have unit volume.

Kernel shape.

The kernel shape is determined by the quadratic form

$$Q_{x_0} = \frac{1}{\sigma^2}\begin{pmatrix} E & F \\ F & G \end{pmatrix} \qquad (2.2)$$

computed from the gradient of I in a neighborhood U of x_0. The diameter of the neighborhood U, called the *window size*, determines the length scale of features "visible" to the filter.

The quadratic form must produce a kernel that is:

1. broad where the gradient is small throughout U, to smooth uniform regions;

2. narrow in the predominant gradient direction where the gradient is large and coherent within U, to smooth along but not across edges, and

3. small and concentrated where the gradient is large in several different directions within U, to preserve corners and triple points.

This is achieved by integrating the gradient components against a weighting function ρ_2:

$$E = \int_U I_x(x)^2 \rho_2(x - x_0)dx,$$

$$F = \int_U I_x(x)I_y(x)\rho_2(x - x_0)dx, \text{ and}$$

$$G = \int_U I_y(x)^2 \rho_2(x - x_0)dx,$$

where $\nabla I = (I_x, I_y)$. ρ_2 is a bump function such as a Gaussian bump that gives more weight to the gradient near x_0.

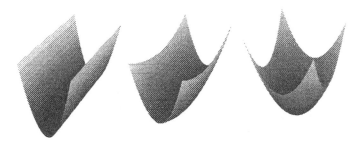

Figure 2.2: 2D plots of quadratic forms, from left to right: at points with strong gradients, the forms correspond to steep parabolic canyons in one direction; Adding them in nearly the same direction gives an elongated paraboloid; Adding them in different directions gives a concentrated paraboloid.

To see that this gives the desired effect, consider the positive semi-definite quadratic form

$$\left(\begin{array}{cc} I_x^2 & I_x I_y \\ I_x I_y & I_y^2 \end{array} \right)$$

at each of the points being integrated. The quadratic form corresponds to a steep canyon aligned perpendicular to the gradient direction, at a point where the gradient is strong, as shown in figure 2.2 (left). Near a straight edge, these are summed for gradients in nearly the same directions. The result is an ellipse elongated in the edge direction and narrowed in the gradient direction with stronger edges giving more eccentric ellipses. Where there are strong gradients in several different directions, the quadratic forms sum to give a small, concentrated ellipse, as shown in figure 2.2 (right). Weak gradients give broad shallow ellipses.

Note that ridges and valleys give the same kernel shape as edges, because Q integrates a quadratic form in ∇I, which is unaffected by a change of sign in ∇I.

Kernel displacement.

Edge enhancement is achieved by displacing the kernel away from nearby edges, so that the filter "brushes" the intensity values on either side of an edge toward the edge. We displace the kernel by a vector $-\alpha(\mathbf{x})$ at each $\mathbf{x}$, so that the intensity values are pushed by $\alpha(\mathbf{x})$.

This is done in such a way as to enhance corners and triple points. For each $\mathbf{x}_0 \in D$ the vector $\alpha(\mathbf{x}_0)$ is computed as a function of the weighted average over a neighborhood U of $\mathbf{x}_0$ of the gradient of I, scaled by its projection, positive or negative, onto the radial direction from $\mathbf{x}_0$:

$$\alpha(\mathbf{x}_0) = \phi(\mathbf{V}),$$

$$\mathbf{V} = \int_U \frac{1}{|\mathbf{y}|} (\nabla I(\mathbf{x}_0 + \mathbf{y}) \cdot \mathbf{y}) \nabla I(\mathbf{x}_0 + \mathbf{y}) \rho_3(\mathbf{y}) d\mathbf{y}, \qquad (2.3)$$

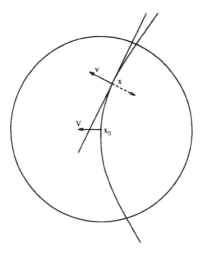

Figure 2.3: Computing $\mathbf{V}$ at a point $\mathbf{x}_0$ on a corner or sharply turning edge. The local contribution of x along one of the edges is perpendicular to the tangent of the edge, in the direction away from $\mathbf{x}_0$. These sum to give a $\mathbf{V}$ pointing outward at the corner, so that the kernel displacement is inward. This gives an enhancement effect by pushing the pixel values outward from the corner.

where ρ_3 is a cut-off function supported on U, c is a constant, and ϕ is a smooth, vector-valued function which compresses the vector $\mathbf{V}$ to limit the displacement. For example, in our implementation $\phi(\mathbf{V}) = c_1\mathbf{V}/\sqrt{\mu^2 + \|\mathbf{V}\|^2}$, with $c_1 \approx (1/4)\cdot$kernel size, and μ is a positive constant.

To see why $\mathbf{V}$ in (2.3) has a desirable effect at corners, we compare it to a more straightforward choice for $\mathbf{V}$,

$$\mathbf{V} = \int_U \|\nabla I(\mathbf{x}_0 + \mathbf{y})\|^2 \mathbf{y} \rho_3(\mathbf{y}) d\mathbf{y}, \qquad (2.4)$$

which measures the first moment of the squared gradient magnitude, to displace the kernel away from strong gradients.

Suppose $\mathbf{x}_0$ is at a corner, and x a neighboring point along one of the edges that comes into the corner (see figure 2.3.) If $\mathbf{V}$ is defined by (2.4), the strong gradient at x affects the first moment of the gradient square, making $\mathbf{V}$ point inward at the corner, which displaces the kernel outward from the corner, resulting in a more rounded corner. On the other hand, for $\mathbf{V}$ defined as in (2.3), the local contribution to $\mathbf{V}$ from x is a vector perpendicular to the local edge direction. Due to the scalar factor $(\nabla I(\mathbf{x}) \cdot \mathbf{y})$, the vector always points away from $\mathbf{x}_0$, so that the local contribution to $\mathbf{V}$ from the different edges make $\mathbf{V}$ point outward from the corner. Thus the kernel is attracted by the corner, and the corner is pushed outward. The effect is to enhance corners and T-junctions, with increasing accuracy at angles near 90 degrees. Experimental results are discussed below (see figure 2.8).

2.1 Nonlinear diffusion

The algorithm as a diffusion process.

The filter algorithm is not inherently a diffusion process; it gives a large effect in one step using certain scale parameters. To express it as a diffusion process, one first considers iterative application of the filter as discrete time evolution, using the output I_{out} of one iteration as the input image I to the next. We then take the limit as the kernel size goes to zero while the window size stays constant, i.e., as σ and ρ_1 are scaled by $\sqrt{\varepsilon}$ ($\varepsilon \approx 0$), and $\alpha = \phi(\mathbf{V})$ is replaced by $\sqrt{\varepsilon}\phi(\sqrt{\varepsilon}\,\mathbf{V})$ to approximate a diffusion equation for time step $\Delta t \approx \varepsilon$ for each iteration[1]. We derive a continuous time evolution by taking the limit as $\varepsilon \to 0$ and $\varepsilon N \to t$, where N is the number of iterations. The result is an integral-differential diffusion equation for the filter, with zero kernel size and finite window size.

Applying the above derivation to equation (2.1) with (2.1') and equation (2.3) yields the evolution equation[2]

$$I_t(\mathbf{x}, t) = \frac{\sigma^2}{4} \sum \left((A\mathbf{Id} + Q)^{-1} \right)_{ij} \nabla_i \nabla_j I(\mathbf{x}, t) - (c_1/\mu)\mathbf{V} \cdot \nabla_\mathbf{x} I(\mathbf{x}, t), \qquad (2.5)$$

where Q is the symmetric matrix corresponding to the quadratic map $Q_{\mathbf{x}_0}: \mathbf{y} \mapsto \mathbf{y}^t Q \mathbf{y}$, $\mathbf{Id}$ is the identity matrix, and A is a constant given by

$$A = \frac{\sigma^2 d\varepsilon}{\int \rho_1^\varepsilon(\mathbf{x})\|\mathbf{x}\|^2 dx} = \frac{\sigma^2 d}{\int \rho_1(\mathbf{x})\|\mathbf{x}\|^2 dx},$$

where d is the dimension of the image domain D. Thus A is the ratio of the smoothing kernel scale σ^2 to a second moment of ρ_1.

To eliminate the integrals in (2.5), we take the limit as the window size goes to zero in Q and in $\mathbf{V}$, i.e., as the support of the cut-off functions ρ_2 and ρ_3 shrinks to a point. As ρ_2 approaches the delta function, the ijth component of $(A\mathbf{Id} + Q)^{-1}$ approaches

$$\frac{1}{A} \left(\delta_{ij} - \frac{1}{A + \|\nabla I\|^2} \nabla_i I \nabla_j I \right).$$

The leading term for $\mathbf{V}$ as the support of ρ_3 shrinks to a point is

$$c \sum_i \nabla_i (\nabla_i I \nabla I), \qquad (2.6)$$

---

[1]Scaling ρ_1 by $\sqrt{\varepsilon}$ here means $\rho_1(\mathbf{x})$ is replaced by $\rho_1^\varepsilon(\mathbf{x}) = \frac{1}{\varepsilon^{d/2}}\rho_1(\frac{\mathbf{x}}{\sqrt{\varepsilon}})$, where d is the dimension of the image domain, so that the total mass of ρ_1^ε is constant. The range of α should then be also scaled by $\sqrt{\varepsilon}$, but since α drifts the heat rather than diffuses it, its effect accumulates linearly in time. Thus we also scale the argument of ϕ by $\sqrt{\varepsilon}$ to get the overall scaling by the factor ε.

[2]Appendix A gives the derivation. Note also that due to the scaling of the argument of ϕ, as $\varepsilon \to 0$ all but the leading term in the Taylor expansion of ϕ have no effect in the limit as $\varepsilon \to 0$, as seen on (2.5).

where

$$c = \frac{1}{d} \int |\mathbf{y}| \rho_3(\mathbf{y}) d\mathbf{y}.$$

So the right way to scale ρ_3 is to keep c constant, i.e.,

$$\rho_3^{\varepsilon'}(\mathbf{y}) = (1/\varepsilon')^{d+1} \rho_3(\mathbf{y}/\varepsilon'), \qquad \varepsilon' > 0.$$

Then $\mathbf{V}$ will approach the quantity in (2.6) as $\varepsilon' \to 0$. So equation (2.5) approaches

$$\frac{\partial I}{\partial t} = \frac{\sigma^2}{4} \frac{1}{A} \left(\Delta I - \frac{\sum \nabla_i I \nabla_j I \nabla_i \nabla_j I}{A + \|\nabla I\|^2} \right) - (cc_1/\mu) \left(\sum_i \nabla_i (\nabla_i I \nabla I) \right) \cdot \nabla I. \quad (2.7)$$

In the one dimensional case, (2.7) reduces to

$$I_t = \zeta(I_x) \cdot I_{xx}, \qquad \text{with} \qquad \zeta(u) = \frac{\sigma^2}{4(A + u^2)} - Cu^2, \; C = 2cc_1/\mu.$$

This is just a heat equation with variable coefficient. Time evolution gives forward heat flow when $\zeta(I_x) > 0$, and backward heat flow otherwise. If we let

$$K = \sqrt{(\sqrt{A^2 + \sigma^2/C} - A)/2},$$

then since $\zeta(u) \lesseqgtr 0$ as $|u| \gtreqless K$ respectively, a suitably regularized version of equation (2.7) will enhance edges where $\|\nabla I\|$ exceeds K.

The idea of casting adaptive smoothing in terms of nonlinear diffusion was recently addressed by Perona and Malik [37]. Their method allows an image $I(\mathbf{x})$ to evolve over time via the diffusion equation

$$I_t(\mathbf{x}, t) = \nabla \cdot D(\mathbf{x}, t) I = D(\mathbf{x}, t) \Delta I + \nabla D \cdot \nabla I, \quad (2.8)$$

where I_t denotes the time derivative of the image intensity function, and D is a function that gives a local estimate of edge-ness, for example,

$$D = \frac{1}{1 + (\|\nabla I\|/K)^2}.$$

The result is to diffuse I most where the gradient $\|\nabla I\|$ is smallest, and least where the gradient is largest. As time passes, I is smoothed within regions of uniform intensity, but not between regions. Edges are enhanced due to the smoothing of regions on either side of an edge.

Equation (2.8) is a heat equation with a variable coefficient. At small gradients, time evolution gives the usual forward heat flow, but when $\|\nabla I\| \geq K$, it gives *backward* heat flow. To see this, we rewrite it in the one-dimensional case[3] letting $\eta(u) = u/(1+(u/K)^2)$:

$$I_t = (\eta(I_x))_x = \eta'(I_x)I_{xx} = \left(\frac{1 - I_x^2/K^2}{(1 + I_x^2/K^2)^2} \right) I_{xx}. \qquad (2.9)$$

This gives forward heat flow when $|I_x| < K$, and backward heat flow otherwise.

Backward heat flow is known to be unstable. Even when the initial function $I(\mathbf{x}, 0)$ is smooth, equation (2.8) *may have no solution even locally in time.* This gives rise to several problems even in the discrete case.

The root of these problems is that the limiting equation (2.8) of the discrete equations is ill-posed as the grid size approaches zero. Thus, the maximum principle proved in [37] cannot be used to show stronger regularity estimates via a bootstrap argument, and the solutions to the discrete equations may have no limit. Even if such a limit exists, it may not be a solution to the limiting equation.

As a result, one cannot reduce the grid size to eliminate discrete lattice artifacts without affecting performance. An edge may be sharpened into one *shock* (i.e., like a step edge) using one grid size, while on a finer grid it may give rise to several shocks. We have observed this in careful one-dimensional simulations, discussed below. Perona and Malik's implementation shows preference to edges aligned with the grid axes, because it updates each point based on nearest neighbor gradients. Such an algorithm will produce a square from a blurred circle and will not improve with a finer grid size.

Moreover, while a fixed grid imposes implicit smoothing, and hence gives a regularization of the equation, it is essential to regularize the limiting equation itself in order to understand and control the behavior of discrete approximations. Thus we want to study modified versions of (2.8), which we will henceforth call the Perona-Malik diffusion equation, where solutions are guaranteed to exist, and which are independent of the choice of grid or other discretization. Equation (2.5) is a better approximation to our filter algorithm because it has a finite window size.

The important conceptual distinction between our algorithm and a grid-simulation of (2.8) is this: while the latter computes a weighted average of nearest neighbors on a grid based on nearest-neighbor gradients, the former makes explicit the shape and size of the weighting function. The weighting function is itself based on gradients in a neighborhood of specific shape and size which are set independent of the grid size. As a result, each iteration of the Perona-Malik simulation is fast and has a small effect, while each iteration of our filter takes more time, but can have a large effect at an explicitly chosen length scale.

One-dimensional simulations.

We study two regularizations of the Perona-Malik diffusion equation. First we write equation (2.8) as

$$I_t = \text{div}(D \, \nabla I),$$

---

[3]The one-dimensional case is meaningful since near a blurred straight edge, a two-dimensional image approximates a function of one variable.

with heat conduction coefficient $D = 1/(1 + \|\nabla I\|^2/K^2)$, and then change D to make it vary smoothly and slowly. To this end, we introduce a new dependent variable v by $D = 1/(1 + v/K^2)$ and describe v as a smoothed version of $\|\nabla I\|^2$ in one of the following two ways:

$$v_t = \omega(\rho * \|\nabla I\|^2 - v), \tag{2.10}$$

$$v_t = \omega\left(\|\nabla I\|^2 - v + \frac{\sigma^2}{2}\Delta v\right), \tag{2.11}$$

where ω and σ are positive scalar parameters, $\rho(\mathbf{x}) = (1/(\sqrt{2\pi}\sigma))^d \exp(-|\mathbf{x}|^2/(2\sigma^2))$, and $*$ denotes convolution in the x-variable(s). Equation (2.10) puts a fixed amount of spatial smoothing on all of $\|\nabla I\|^2$, while in (2.11) the last term on the right hand side makes the "older" $\|\nabla I\|^2$ more diffused.

In either case, σ is the amount of the spatial smoothing, and ω^{-1} is the average time delay. Perona-Malik's equation ($v = \|\nabla I\|^2$) may be recovered by taking $\sigma \to 0$, then $\omega \to \infty$.

Letting $\sigma \to 0$, we obtain the average time delay of $1/\omega$ with no spatial smoothing:

$$v(\mathbf{x}, t) = \exp(-\omega t)v(\mathbf{x}, 0) + \omega \int_0^t \exp(-\omega(t - s))\|\nabla I\|^2(\mathbf{x}, s)ds.$$

For the general σ and ω, similar formulas can be obtained by using Green's function for the homogeneous linear equation corresponding to (2.10) or (2.11).

In the 1-d case, the modified Perona-Malik equation is thus

$$I_t = \left(\frac{I_x}{1 + v/K^2}\right)_x, \qquad v_t = \omega(\rho(x) * I_x^2 - v) \tag{2.12}$$

if v is given by (2.10), and

$$I_t = \left(\frac{I_x}{1 + v/K^2}\right)_x, \qquad v_t = \omega\left((I_x^2 - v) + \frac{\sigma^2}{2}v_{xx}\right) \tag{2.13}$$

if v is given by (2.11).

Our simulations begin with an initial function $I(x, 0)$ on the interval $[0, 1]$ that represents a blurred edge in one dimension. We chose $I(x, 0) = 140 \int (x(1 - x))^3 dx = 35x^4 - 84x^5 + 70x^6 - 20x^7$, shown in figure 2.4a, because it is steepest in the middle of the $[0, 1]$ interval and almost flat at both ends. The factor 140 makes $I(1, 0) = 1$. We take a suitable initial value for v, e.g., a smoothed version of $|I'(x, 0)|^2$, and assume no heat conduction through the boundary. We use Crank-Nicholson's algorithm [9] with a variable grid size, subdivided when dI exceeds a given $\varepsilon > 0$, and a variable time step ($dt \leq \tau \max((dx)^2/D)$ for a given $\tau > 0$) to solve the first equation in (2.12) and both equations in (2.13).

Our numerical simulations lead to several observations. As $\sigma \to 0$ and $\omega \to \infty$, that is, as the equation approaches the Perona-Malik equation, I changes drastically after a very short time, creating many discontinuities in the unstable region $\{x \mid |I'(x, 0)| > K\}$. This blocks the heat flow and thus freezes the shape of the graph of I in the unstable region to a jagged version of the graph of $I(x, 0)$, shown in figure 2.4b. This confirms our

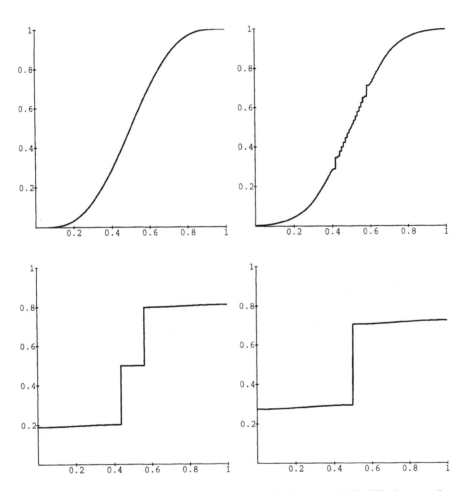

Figure 2.4: One-dimensional simulations of a modified Perona-Malik diffusion equation: *a*, upper-left, The initial function $I(x,0)$; *b*, upper-right, Letting parameters $\sigma \to 0$, $\omega \to \infty$, in order to recover the original Perona-Malik equation, gives this jagged result after a short time; *c*, lower-left, The formation of a double shock from the single edge where K is too small; *d*, lower-right, The formation of a single shock, using a small σ. Both the double and single shocks keep their shape for a relatively long time.

view that a regularization is essential to make the Perona-Malik simulations create shocks gracefully. Perona and Malik observed that at a point on an edge where $\|\nabla I\|$ is at a local maximum in the gradient direction (perpendicular to the edge direction), $\|\nabla I\|$ increases over time. But this does not imply that $\|\nabla I\|$ increases at the center of an S-shaped edge profile such as in figure 2.4a, to form a single shock. Indeed, at such a point $\|\nabla I\|$ could cease to be a local maximum at some time t, after which $\|\nabla I\|$ may start decreasing. This actually occurs in our simulations, with $\sigma = .00005, \omega = 100, K = 1, \varepsilon = .01, \tau = .25$, where $I(x, 0)$ forms two shocks by time $t = .165$ (see figure 2.4c).

When $\sigma > 0$, a shock front forms slowly. Because $\max_x |I_x|$ is bounded by some constant depending on K and σ, the shock front will never be infinitely sharp. This suggests the global existence of a solution when $\sigma > 0$. Indeed, since heat flows through a smeared shock front, the solution would approach a global constant as $t \rightarrow \infty$.

When $\sigma = 0$ so there is no spatial smoothing, a shock forms quickly and $\max_x |I_x|$ grows rapidly in time, making it hard to maintain the accuracy of simulations. But for a fixed $T < \infty$ and small enough $\sigma > 0$, the solution seems to keep its overall shape, similar to the case of $\sigma = 0$ over the time interval of $0 \leq t \leq T$. Also, the number of shocks is controled by ω, although each shock seems to become infinitely sharp.

These suggest the solution exists globally when $\sigma = 0$, although $\max_x |I_x|$ grows rapidly, and as $t \rightarrow \infty$ approaches a step function. Hence equation (2.13) with $\sigma = 0$ in the purely analog world realizes a certain segmentation of the original smooth image.

To make either our filter or a grid-simulation of the Perona-Malik equation effective, one must choose parameter values carefully depending on the scale of geometric features of interest in typical input images. Even with $I(x, 0)$ as above, we have observed a small range of parameters, particularly K, for which only one shock forms. In these instances larger K gives no shock, and smaller K gives more than one shock (see figures 2.4c and 2.4d).

2.2 Experimental results

Our experimental filter program is slower and more complex than might be necessary for practical use. Appendix B gives a programmer's description for a simpler and faster implementation. In both cases, since I_{out} at each point depends on the values of I in a small neighborhood of the point, a program can be optimized for space by operating on a large image in small patches–as small as the neighborhood size. To optimize for speed, intermediate values can be computed in arrays as big as the original I.

Our experimental implementation of the filter algorithm takes parameters σ^2 and μ to tune the eccentricity and displacement of the kernel for "typical" image data; they depend on the distribution of values of ∇I. Our test images are renormalized so that $0 \leq I \leq 255$. The images then typically have mean $\cong 120$ and standard deviation $\cong 50$. Gradient magnitude typically ranges from 0 to 35, with 99 percent of the gradient values falling below 16. (The cameras and digitizers used typically respond to a sharp black/white transition in no less than 6 pixels.)

In our implementation, we have found that $\sigma^2 \cong 100$ and $\mu \cong 100$ work well for images taken from several different digitizers. In the exponential used to build the kernel $e^{-(Ex^2 + 2Fxy + Gy^2)/2\sigma^2}$, E, F and G are computed from the gradient, so σ has units of intensity like I; 100 is the right order of magnitude. From (2.3) we see that μ has units of intensity^2/length^3 like $\mathbf{V}$; it controls the "speed" of kernel displacement as we move $\mathbf{x}_0$ across an edge. The order of μ depends on how steep and strong the edges are that we expect to see in our images. Our strongest observed edges cover about half the intensity range in about 3 pixels, so $\mathbf{V}$ between 100 and 200 near these edges and $\mu = 100$ is on the right order. The choice of these parameters is not critical; they have not required adjustment during the course of hundreds of experiments. M and N, the integer values for the window and kernel sizes in pixel units, are typically between 5 and 15. We precompute

$$\rho_1(\mathbf{x}) = \max\{1 - \frac{|\mathbf{x}|^2}{1 + N(N-1)/2}, 0\},$$

on the $N \times N$ lattice centered at 0, while convolution of I_x^2, $I_x I_y$ and I_y^2 by

$$\rho_2(\mathbf{x}) = \frac{1}{K_2} e^{-8|\mathbf{x}|^2/(M^2+M+1)} \qquad \text{and} \qquad \frac{1}{|\mathbf{x}|} \rho_3(\mathbf{x}) = \frac{1}{K_3} e^{-36|\mathbf{x}|^2/(M^2+M+1)},$$

where

$$K_2 = \sum_{\max(|x|,|y|)<M} e^{-8|\mathbf{x}|^2/(M^2+M+1)} \qquad \text{and} \qquad K_3 = \sum_{\max(|x|,|y|)<M} e^{-36|\mathbf{x}|^2/(M^2+M+1)},$$

are computed separately in the x-variable and then the y-variable on the $2M \times 2M$ lattice centered at 0 to reduce the amount of calculations for large M. The $2M \times 2M$ lattice is used rather than the $M \times M$ lattice to maintain rotational invariance and prevent noise from the sharp cut-off of the tails of ρ_2 and ρ_3.

Alternatively one can use some windowing techniques or spline the tails of the exponentials gracefully to zero to prevent effects of the window edges more efficiently. We used two separate formulas for ρ_2 and ρ_3 to controlling the window size for the kernel shape separately from the window size for the kernel displacement. In practice, one can use the same window size, and hence the same formula for ρ_2 and ρ_3. In this case one can speed up the calculations by using a property of the exponential function, $(d/dx)e^{-x^2} = -2xe^{-x^2}$, which allows one to compute $\mathbf{V}$ simply using derivatives of E, F, and G. See Appendix B for the explicit formulas.

Results on certain test images are shown in figures 2.5–2.7. The filter sharpens edges without preference to particular angles; its effect on a blurred circle confirms this. It can smooth out noise while sharpening somewhat blurred salient edges, as shown in figure 2.6 The effect on T-junctions and corners in a real image can be seen in figure 2.7.

Figure 2.8 shows how the filter behaves at ideal corners and T-junctions. It shows a corner, a right angle T-junction, and an oblique T-junction, blurred with a Gaussian kernel, and then sharpened by the filter. The third row down shows the effect of the filter using a displacement term that rounds corners, given by (2.4). The fourth row shows the one that enhances corners, given by (2.3). The enhanced corner is widened and rounded by the process, and is displaced slightly inward from the center. The right angle T-junction is beautifully restored. The oblique T-junction is displaced downward because of distortion due to the nearby stronger edge.

We have also observed two important properties of the filter. When the input image I

Figure 2.5: The filter applied to a blurred circular Gaussian bump produces a circle. ($M = N = 11, \sigma^2 = \mu = 100$, iterated 4 times.)

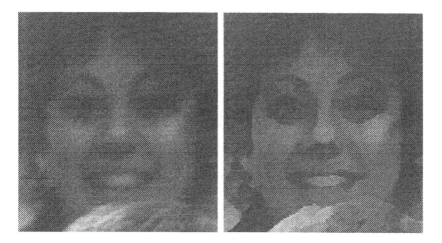

Figure 2.6: Applied to a blurred, noisy image of a face, the filter sharpens salient edges and eliminates noise from uniform regions. Note the corners of the mouth are enhanced (2 iterations.)

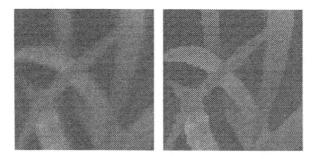

Figure 2.7: The filter applied to a an image of blades of grass with natural corners and T-junctions. The grid is visible due to the low resolution of the original (2 iterations.)

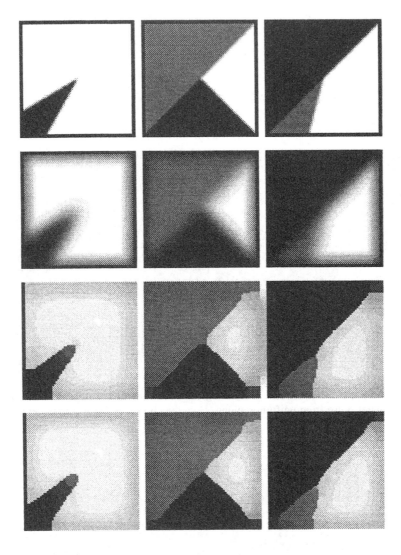

Figure 2.8: The effect of the filter on ideal corners and T-junctions. From the top: original images; images after blurring with a Gaussian of standard deviation 3.75; output of the filter with the displacement term V defined as in formula (2.4); output with V defined as in formula (2.3); $M = N = 7, \sigma^2 = \mu = 100$, 20 iterations.

contains random noise, the resulting random fluctuations of ∇I add up to make Q more positive, which reduces smoothing within regions. Thus a local noise estimate is needed to compensate.

If I is the sum of the "signal" I_S and the "noise" I_N, and if, for any i and j, $\partial I_S/\partial x_i$ is locally almost L^2-perpendicular to $\partial I_N/\partial x_j$ (for example if I_S is a smeared picture and I_N is a random noise with little low frequency content), then the kernel constructed from I is almost the product of the kernels constructed from I_S and from I_N. Thus if I_N is random noise with no preferred direction, it simply makes the effective kernel size smaller.

To see this, observe that

$$
\begin{aligned}
Q_{\mathbf{x}_0}(\mathbf{y}) &= \int \rho_2(\xi - \mathbf{x}_0)(\nabla(I_S(\xi) + I_N(\xi)) \cdot \mathbf{y})^2 d\xi \\
&\cong \int \rho_2(\xi - \mathbf{x}_0)(\nabla I_S(\xi) \cdot \mathbf{y})^2 d\xi + \int \rho_2(\xi - \mathbf{x}_0)(\nabla I_N(\xi) \cdot \mathbf{y})^2 d\xi \quad (2.14) \\
&=: Q_S(\mathbf{y}) + Q_N(\mathbf{y}),
\end{aligned}
$$

because $\partial I_S/\partial x_i$ is almost perpendicular $\partial I_N/\partial x_j$,

$$
e^{-Q_{\mathbf{x}_0}/\sigma^2} \cong e^{-Q_S/\sigma^2} e^{-Q_N/\sigma^2}.
$$

If I_N is a random noise with no preferred direction, then the second factor on the right hand side of this formula approximates a Gaussian bump and makes the effective kernel size smaller.

To cope with this problem, in our implementation of the filter we have an optional Gaussian smoothing before computing Q. This solves the problem if ∇I_N consists mainly of high frequency components. After computing the kernel k, the input I is fed directly into the right hand side of (2.1) without extra smoothing, since I appears there only linearly, so that random noise with little low frequency component will have little effect on the result. When the filter is applied iteratively, the auxiliary smoothing is performed only on the first pass, because:

- The smoothing is not needed after the first pass since the filter reduces noise;

- Ridges and valleys are weakened by smoothing even more so than edges, hence we cannot make the kernel compressed enough to preserve them when smoothed. Since ridges and valleys are not enhanced by the kernel displacement the smoothing will weaken them further.

Secondly, the filter has a tendency to eat thin ridges and valleys, because it sharpens edges by thinning them. The effect can be reduced by blurring I before using its gradient to compute α.

2.3 Using Q for corner detection

Although the filter was originally developed as a preprocessing stage for edge, corner, and triple point detection, the intermediate information for computing the kernel may be used for a more integrated approach to these detection tasks. The mechanisms that shrink and displace the kernel at corners are useful for corner detection. For example, local maxima of the determinant of the quadratic form Q correspond well to corners (See figure 3.6). This is less sensitive to noise and better in locating blurred corners than extrema of the determinant of the Hessian, used by Nagel [30]. Its location is displaced outward in the direction of the axis of the symmetry of a corner, an effect similar to human perception, rather than being displaced sideways, as often happens to extrema of the determinant of the Hessian.

The method is also related to Kitchen and Rosenfeld's corner detector [19], which seeks points of maximal 1-dimensional curvature of a level curve through each point on strong edges, scaled by the magnitude of the gradient of I. This corresponds to extrema, along edges, of the second directional derivative in the edge direction, i.e.,

$$\frac{1}{\|\nabla I\|^2}(-I_y, I_x) \begin{pmatrix} I_{xx} & I_{xy} \\ I_{xy} & I_{yy} \end{pmatrix} \begin{pmatrix} -I_y \\ I_x \end{pmatrix}. \tag{2.15}$$

Somewhat remarkably, a similar quantity

$$\left\| \begin{pmatrix} I_{xx} & I_{xy} \\ I_{xy} & I_{yy} \end{pmatrix} \begin{pmatrix} -I_y \\ I_x \end{pmatrix} \right\|^2 = (-I_y, I_x) \begin{pmatrix} I_{xx} & I_{xy} \\ I_{xy} & I_{yy} \end{pmatrix}^2 \begin{pmatrix} -I_y \\ I_x \end{pmatrix} \tag{2.16}$$

appears as the coefficient of the leading term in an asymptotic expansion of the determinant of Q, as the window size goes to zero.

To see this, recall that ρ_2 is rotationally symmetric, so that its first moments as well as $\int \rho_2(x, y)xy \, dxdy$ vanish, and let

$$\varepsilon = \int \rho_2(x, y)x^2/2 \, dxdy = \int \rho_2(x, y)y^2/2 \, dxdy.$$

As the window size goes to zero, ρ_2 is scaled so that it keeps the unit volume, while $\varepsilon \to 0$, and a higher moment approaches zero at a higher order in ε. Thus by the Taylor expansions of $(I_x)^2$, $I_x I_y$ and $(I_y)^2$, we have

$$Q = \int \begin{pmatrix} (I_x)^2 & I_x I_y \\ I_x I_y & (I_y)^2 \end{pmatrix}(\mathbf{x})\rho_2(\mathbf{x} - \mathbf{x}_0)d\mathbf{x}$$

$$= (1 + \varepsilon\Delta) \begin{pmatrix} (I_x)^2 & I_x I_y \\ I_x I_y & (I_y)^2 \end{pmatrix}(\mathbf{x}_0) + o(\varepsilon),$$

where $\Delta = (\partial/\partial x)^2 + (\partial/\partial y)^2$. Therefore by using

$$\det \begin{pmatrix} (I_x)^2 & I_x I_y \\ I_x I_y & (I_y)^2 \end{pmatrix} = 0,$$

$$0 = \left(\frac{\partial}{\partial x}\right)^2 \det \begin{pmatrix} (I_x)^2 & I_x I_y \\ I_x I_y & (I_y)^2 \end{pmatrix}$$

$$= \det \begin{pmatrix} ((I_x)^2)_{xx} & I_x I_y \\ (I_x I_y)_{xx} & (I_y)^2 \end{pmatrix} + \det \begin{pmatrix} (I_x)^2 & (I_x I_y)_{xx} \\ I_x I_y & ((I_y)^2)_{xx} \end{pmatrix}$$

$$+ 2 \det \begin{pmatrix} ((I_x)^2)_x & (I_x I_y)_x \\ (I_x I_y)_x & ((I_y)^2)_x \end{pmatrix}$$

and a similar identity for $\partial/\partial y$, we have

$$\det Q = \varepsilon \left[\det \begin{pmatrix} \Delta((I_x)^2) & I_x I_y \\ \Delta(I_x I_y) & (I_y)^2 \end{pmatrix} + \det \begin{pmatrix} (I_x)^2 & \Delta(I_x I_y) \\ I_x I_y & \Delta((I_y)^2) \end{pmatrix} \right] + o(\varepsilon)$$

$$= -2\varepsilon \left[\det \begin{pmatrix} ((I_x)^2)_x & (I_x I_y)_x \\ (I_x I_y)_x & ((I_y)^2)_x \end{pmatrix} + \det \begin{pmatrix} ((I_x)^2)_y & (I_x I_y)_y \\ (I_x I_y)_y & ((I_y)^2)_y \end{pmatrix} \right] + o(\varepsilon)$$

$$= -2\varepsilon \left[\det \begin{pmatrix} 2 I_x I_{xx} & I_{xx} I_y + I_x I_{xy} \\ I_{xx} I_y + I_x I_{xy} & 2 I_y I_{xy} \end{pmatrix} \right.$$

$$\left. + \det \begin{pmatrix} 2 I_x I_{xy} & I_{xy} I_y + I_x I_{yy} \\ I_{xy} I_y + I_x I_{yy} & 2 I_y I_{yy} \end{pmatrix} \right] + o(\varepsilon)$$

$$= 2\varepsilon \left((I_{xx} I_y - I_{xy} I_x)^2 + (I_{xy} I_y - I_{yy} I_x)^2 \right) + o(\varepsilon)$$

This last expression contains 2.16 as the coefficient of the leading term.

Since the quadratic form Q comes up naturally in the filter algorithm to measure the variation of edge directions in a neighborhood, one may omit the edge detection stage and simply compute the quantity in 2.15 the determinant of Q, or its first approximation 2.16, over the whole image.

Figures 2.9–2.12 are those and some related quantities computed over a Gaussian-blurred corner image. They indicate that the peaks over the whole neighborhood of the quantities 2.15 and 2.16 indeed locate corners quite well, compared with Hessian-based quantities which tend to produce a pair of peaks on both sides of the tip of the corner.

Other features can be detected using the filter's intermediate computations. The quadratic quantities I_x^2 and I_y^2 have been used to measure verticality and horizontality in *kanji* (Chinese character) recognition, where vertical and horizontal strokes are predominant. One can represent the square of any directional derivative by a linear combination of these and $I_x I_y$. Thus the triple $(I_x^2, I_x I_y, I_y^2)$ computed by the filter gives rotationally symmetric data, with which the techniques developed for kanji recognition would apply to more general pattern recognition problems. Freeman and Adelson have done a more general study of this type of filter that gives a measure for all directions by linear combinations, which they call steerable filters [11].

Figure 2.9: The initial corner image $I(x, y)$: an ideal corner that sweeps out 50° of arc, 201 × 201 pixels, blurred with a gaussian of standard deviation 20.

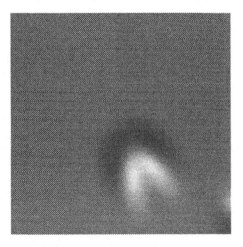

Figure 2.10: The determinant of the Hessian of I multiplied by $\|\nabla I\|^2$ to give it the same dimensions as 2.16. Black is negative and white is positive. Note that there are two peaks and two dips, so the corner is not well localized.

Figure 2.11: Left, The quantity given by the square of 2.15. Right, Same, except that the normalization factor $1/\|\nabla I\|^2$ is replaced by $1/\|\nabla I\|$ in order to give it the same dimensions as 2.16. There is one elongated peak in each, with less elongation in the image on the right. Kitchen and Rosenfeld's algorithm intersects this with the edge defined by non-maximum supression, which gives good localization of the corner.

Figure 2.12: The quantity given by 2.16. As noted, it is remarkably similar to the right hand image of figure 2.11.

Chapter 3

Finding Contours and Junctions

The problem of finding lines and edges in images has been pursued vigorously since the early 1960s, and has a still burgeoning literature. The earliest methods for segmenting digital pictures into regions were based on thresholding, i.e., cutting the domain D along curves where $I = k_1, k_2, \ldots$ for some threshold values k_i. These methods still prevail in the medical, manufacturing and test equipment areas, and notably, for character recognition. This would suffice for a first stage in case we were designing a system for a specific task which involved images of several known intensities. One such task might be to reconstruct the traces of a printed circuit card which are partly overlaid with silkscreened letters. Under suitably controlled lighting, the three types of surface—board, trace, and silkscreened letter—will reflect three disjoint ranges of brightness or color.

Somewhat more general purpose methods for edge-finding are based on finding lines of high contrast. The first such schemes characterized step-edges as first or second derivatives, and tried to find optimal estimators of these for digital pictures over some small support. Most often cited in this context are the methods of Marr and Hildreth [23], which used the zero curves of the Laplacian of a broad Gaussian because it provided a good compromise of localization and bandwidth, and Canny [5], who combined several local maxima criteria with hysteresis to extend strong edges along weak stretches.

These two algorithms have become de facto standards against which other contrast-based edge-detectors are measured. Our algorithm uses the local maxima criteria and hysteresis principle used in Canny's algorithm, but begins with a more general and robust edge operator which responds to ridges and valleys as well as to light/dark transitions. Generalized edge/line finding operators as well as junction (also called keypoint) detectors have been proposed more recently by Perona [38], Rosenthaler *et al* [40], and Freeman [10]. Our edge operator yields a vector field like the gradient that gives edge strength and direction, computed from the quadratic form Q of the previous chapter. Because Q is a quadratic form in the gradient components, edge strength has peaks at thin ridges and valleys in addition to step edges of the intensity function. Edge direction is the maximal direction of mean square directional derivative computed over a neighborhood, rather than the maximal direction of mean magnitude of gradient.

Our objective is to find and represent the contours $\Gamma = \{\gamma_1, \cdots, \gamma_k\}$ that correspond to the visible portions of object outlines. We reiterate the crucial point that high-contrast lines are generally bad guesses at the real locations of object outlines. To compensate we must exclude from Γ crucial elements of practically all scenes that reach our eyes, including texture, shading, and shadow boundaries. Even if we restrict input to pictures taken on foggy or overcast days, or to indoor scenes with the most even lighting possible, there are many contrast edges which do not correspond to object outlines and object outlines not manifest in the image as contrast edges.

The later stages of processing require knowing the location, length, curvature, and tangent along contours. The data structure for a contour γ must give:

1. a way to find locations of successive points along the contour, for "rendering" it on a discrete lattice, and for labeling regions in a sampled image;

2. a way to evaluate its length $\int_\gamma ds$;

3. a way to evaluate its total curvature squared $\int_\gamma \kappa^2 ds$;

4. the tangents at the endpoints $\dot{\gamma}(0)$ and $\dot{\gamma}(1)$; and

5. a way to find the locations where a new contour $\gamma' \notin \Gamma$ intersects one or more $\gamma \in \Gamma$, if indeed it intersects any.

To handle a variety of objects, it is not feasible to approximate an entire contour γ by one polynomial, even one of high order. We must segment contours into shorter, simpler pieces.

It turns out that the simplest kind of pieces–line segments–suffices for our purpose. We store γ as a set of points together with a tangent angle and curvature at each point, i.e., $(x_i, y_i, \theta_i, \kappa_i)_\gamma, 1 \leq n_\gamma$. This is similar in spirit to the work of Zucker et al [7]. Since the locations of points on a grid that approximate a curve can vary by half a distance unit from the actual curve in $\mathbf{R}^2$, we use ten or more points at a time when approximating tangent and curvature. This is treated below as part of the problem of curve smoothing.

3.1   Finding edges

Recall from the previous chapter that the quadratic form computed at each $\mathbf{x}_0$ in the image domain U,

$$\begin{pmatrix} E & F \\ F & G \end{pmatrix}, \text{ with}$$

$$E = \int_U I_x(\mathbf{x})^2 \rho_2(\mathbf{x} - \mathbf{x}_0) d\mathbf{x},$$

$$F = \int_U I_x(\mathbf{x}) I_y(\mathbf{x}) \rho_2(\mathbf{x} - \mathbf{x}_0) d\mathbf{x}, \text{ and}$$

$$G = \int_U I_y(\mathbf{x})^2 \rho_2(\mathbf{x} - \mathbf{x}_0) d\mathbf{x},$$

captures gradient strength and coherence information in a neighborhood of $\mathbf{x}_0$ that depends on the effective support of the weighting function ρ_2. Our implementation uses an approximate Gaussian weighting function for ρ_2, described below. The eigenvalues $0 \leq \lambda_1 < \lambda_2$ and their corresponding eigenvectors $\mathbf{v}_1$ and $\mathbf{v}_2$ can be read as follows:

- The eigenvalues of the matrix, λ_1 and λ_2, are weighted means of square gradient in maximal and minimal directions, so the square root of the trace of the matrix $\sqrt{\lambda_1 + \lambda_2} = \sqrt{\int \|\nabla I\|^2 \rho_2 d\mathbf{x}}$ can be used as a measure of edge strength.

- The larger eigenvalue λ_2 is like the weighted mean square of gradient in the direction in which it is maximal. Since a strong gradient is perpendicular to an edge, $\mathbf{v}_2$ is perpendicular to the edge direction when the gradients are predominantly similar in direction. Because the matrix is symmetric, $\mathbf{v}_1$ thus approximates edge direction at each point.

- λ_1 is like a weighted variance of gradient directions in the neighborhood, so it will increase as there are strong gradients in different directions. Like $detQ = \lambda_1 \lambda_2$ considered in section 2.3, λ_1 itself can be used as a measure of cornerness.

The input image is a discrete sampled array $I(x,y)$, $x \in \{0, \ldots, \text{width} - 1\}$, $y \in \{0, \ldots, \text{height} - 1\}$, as in the simple filter algorithm. A parameter σ, in distance units, determines the width of the effective support of the blurring kernels and several other length scale variables. All arrays, including the input image and variables are stored in IEEE standard single-precision floating point format. The edge tracing algorithm is as follows:

Compute edge strength, edge direction, and cornerness

We begin by building the three arrays, $E(x,y)$, $F(x,y)$, and $G(x,y)$, containing blurred versions of I_x^2, $I_x I_y$ and I_y^2 respectively. This is described more fully in Appendix B.

Next, we create three arrays to hold edge strength, edge direction and cornerness computed from the quadratic form as described above. Let $\lambda_1(x,y) < \lambda_2(x,y)$ be the eigenvalues and $\mathbf{v}_1(x,y)$ and $\mathbf{v}_2(x,y)$ be the corresponding eigenvectors of the matrix

$$\begin{pmatrix} E(x,y) & F(x,y) \\ F(x,y) & G(x,y) \end{pmatrix}$$

computed at each point (x,y). Then we build new arrays for the edge strength $s(x,y)$, edge direction $\theta(x,y)$, and cornerness $c(x,y)$ as follows:

$$\begin{aligned} s(x,y) &:= \sqrt{\lambda_1 + \lambda_2} \\ \theta(x,y) &:= \arg(\mathbf{v}_1) \\ c(x,y) &:= \lambda_1 \end{aligned}$$

where $\arg(\mathbf{v}) = \tan^{-1}(\mathbf{v}_y / \mathbf{v}_x)$. Note that $\theta(x,y)$ is defined modulo π.

Trace edges to form initial contour point lists

To trace strong edges across weak stretches, we use a hysteresis with one low and one high threshold chosen for the entire image. These are computed as the 30th and 60th percentiles of the edge-strength array, i.e., the 30th percentile value is chosen so that for 30 percent of the points (x,y), $s(x,y)$ is below that value. (The actual percentiles are parameters, but no variation has been needed to achieve the modest performance for the images used in our simulations.)

The tracing begins with the number of contours $k = 0$. For each pixel (x, y) not yet part of a contour, if $s(x, y) >$ high-threshold and if the pixel is a local maximum in the edge-strength field in the directions perpendicular to the edge direction, we build a one-point contour by incrementing k and putting $(x, y, \theta(x, y), 0)$ on the list of points for γ_k (curvature is not estimated at this time). We then build γ_k by tracing the edge, adding successive points, heading first in one direction along the edge at (x, y), and then in the other.

Build γ_k by adding successive points.

We define a rule for finding the best candidate neighbor among the eight nearest neighbors of (x, y) to continue the contour. Only candidates with edge-strength $>$ low-threshold, and which are local maxima in the edge-strength field in the directions perpendicular to their edge direction, are qualified for the competition. Canny called this "non-maximum suppression." If there are no qualifying candidate neighbors, the curve γ_k ends at (x, y). If γ_k has at least two points, then candidate neighbors must not introduce an acute angle; i.e., the trajectory from the previous to the current point must form an angle of at least 90 degrees with the trajectory from the current point to the candidate.

Preference is given to nearer neighbors whose edge-direction more closely matches the edge direction at (x, y). Thus a penalty measure for a candidate (x', y') to succeed a point (x, y) in γ can be defined as

$$\text{match-penalty}_{(x,y)}(x', y') = \sin(|\theta(x, y) - \theta(x', y')|) + c\|(x, y) - (x', y')\|,$$

where $c = \sin(15°)$. A diagonal point like $(x - 1, y - 1)$ beats a compass point like $(x - 1, y)$ only if its edge direction is at least 6.2 degrees closer to the edge direction at (x, y). As long as the candidates meet the low threshold, their edge strengths do not play a role in the competition. This is because larger gradients do not in general make more important edges as we trace object outlines.

Having once found the candidate (x_2, y_2) with least match-penalty, we treat it as follows:

- If (x_2, y_2) is not part of an existing contour, then we add $(x_2, y_2, \theta(x_2, y_2), 0)$ to the end of γ_k and continue by finding a candidate neighbor of (x_2, y_2). Otherwise, we have hit a contour point, and will stop tracing the edge in one of three ways.

- If (x_2, y_2) is an endpoint of a different contour γ_i, then replace γ_i by a new contour made up of the combination of the two, and decrement the number of contours k.

- If (x_2, y_2) is the other end of γ_k, then we mark γ_k a closed contour.

- If the best candidate neighbor belongs to another contour γ_i, then γ_k ends there, and γ_i is split into two contours at that point, which now becomes a triple point. In case $i = k$, a closed contour is formed. In either case, splitting γ_i introduces a new contour, so k in incremented.

A contour may not run into itself too close to the growing endpoint, lest it form an impossibly small region. Any point on the contour that is too close to the end being built is disqualified as a candidate. The implementation defines "too close" as 4σ, counting the number of points from the growing end to the self-intersect.

When all points have been visited, curves of only one point are deleted, resulting in a set of chain-coded curves $\Gamma = \{\gamma_1, \cdots, \gamma_k\}$. Figure 3.1 shows the initial contours found by applying the algorithm to our still life. Far from ideal, the algorithm detects the lettering in the background rather poorly, and leaves junctions incomplete. Although the lighting is even, the slight shadows at the bottom already lead the edges at the bottom of the potato outward. This is a limitation to using brightness gradients alone without special treatment for shadows. Note also that there are small gaps even n strong edges, for example on the right side of the potato, where the texture of one surface causes accidental matches with a neighboring surface.

Jump gaps

This edge-detection technique is really designed to find one-dimensional edges, ie. features consisting of a blurred step edge in one direction, constant in the orthogonal direction. It leaves gaps not only along boundaries between slightly textured regions, but also at junctions. David Beymer [1] gave a thorough treatment of this problem with gradient-based edge detectors, and proposed a fix based on the profile of the gradient magnitude near T-junctions.

In the current algorithm, we solve the problem with a simple heuristic; we discuss alternative methods in the concluding chapter. Gap-jumping is conceptually the same operation as building the "continuations" of the following chapter. We use this separate operation here to compensate for the small gaps and incomplete junctions left after tracing contours. The simple solution is to grow contours at their endpoints by reflecting in the line that passes through the endpoint perpendicular to the observed edge direction at or near the endpoint (figure 3.2). Exactly at an endpoint, the mean square gradient in a neighborhood does not always yield a strong edge due either to nearby edges in different directions, or simply due to the drop below the low threshold. Thus the edge direction at endpoints may be unreliable. To compensate, we move back along the contour by 2σ and take the edge direction at that point instead of at the endpoint. This is still not completely reliable–the edge direction after all depends on a neighborhood, which may contain other edges. We also vary the angle of reflection a small amount–$\pm 15°$–in case the endpoint does not grow to meet nearby contours.

On a rectangular lattice with 8-connected contours, diagonal portions of contours can cross over each other without colliding at any grid point. To assure collision, each time a contour grows by one point, the five neighbors that agree with the growth trajectory are checked as well.

The reflected points almost never fall on grid points. It is best to store real coordinate values (x, y), and to insert extra points where needed to keep the lattice-point path of γ eight-connected. The lattice point corresponding to $(x, y) \in \mathbf{R}^2$ is $(\lfloor x + 0.5 \rfloor, \lfloor y + 0.5 \rfloor)$, so that the area associated to the point with integer coordinates (a, b) is as shown in figure 3.4.

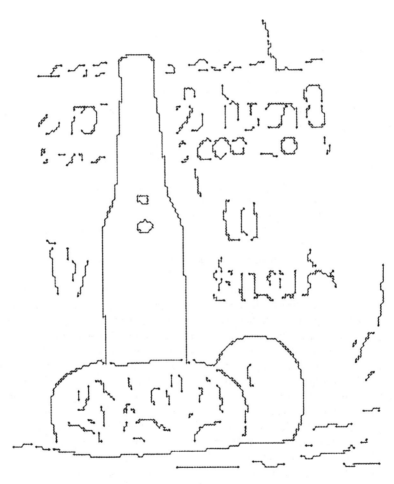

Figure 3.1: The result of the initial edge tracing algorithm on figure 0.1 with $\sigma = 1.25$. Successive points on the same contour are connected by thin line segments. Thicker segments indicate edge direction at each point. Endpoints are marked by circles; nonendpoints by dots.

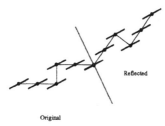

Figure 3.2: Extending a contour by reflecting in the line that passes through the endpoint perpendicular to the tangent to the edge near the endpoint.

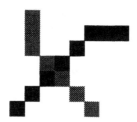

Figure 3.3: Diagonal portions of contours can cross over each other without colliding at any grid point.

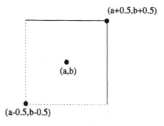

Figure 3.4: The area in $\mathbf{R}^2$ that corresponds to grid point (a, b).

Figure 3.5 shows the results of applying this growth procedure to the still life. This method puts the problem of finding junctions after that of tracing edges. In fact, the cornerness measure $c(x,y)$ also has strong responses at junctions. Its application in a junction detector alone is left for future investigations. Figure 3.6 shows the cornerness array (darker is stronger), the smaller eigenvalue of the symmetric matrix $\begin{pmatrix} E & F \\ F & G \end{pmatrix}$, for the still life picture.

Delete crack tips and short contours

Recall that we will ultimately be working with a piecewise constant model, so crack tips will be ignored in the last stages. One may therefore delete any contour with a stray end, that is, any contour not connected to other contours at both ends. Closed contours of fewer than a certain fixed number of points may also be deleted. Figure 3.7 shows the result of deleting crack tips and short contours.

The result is a delicate edge tracing stage. An important edge with a gap just one pixel longer than the gap-jumping threshold length will be deleted entirely from Γ during the pruning step. In the future, the algorithm should be made more robust by adaptively setting the thresholds and σ. In our experiments the maximum growth length is 3.2σ. This is increased for pictures where textured regions or shadows lead the contour tracer astray.

3.2   Finding corners and T-junctions

The edge maps shown in the previous figures are built on grid points, and are therefore jagged. From these we want to infer smooth contours, without rounding off real corners, or changing the overall sizes and shapes of regions.

This problem arises whenever computer applications use "real" image data, i.e., images stored as 2-dimensional arrays rather than in a higher-level geometric form. In computer publishing, line drawings and photos are the real data used for newspaper and magazine ads. To manipulate the electronic images, for example to crop, rotate and scale them, it is important to remove grid artifacts from the representation of object outlines; that is, to infer curves that are smooth except at "corner" points.

At the time of this writing, a major supplier of digitized fonts still created geometric descriptions manually from large printed exemplars of individual letters [2]. Here, corner-detection means quantitatively capturing the font designer's aesthetic judgement. It is also difficult to choose a representation which yields the right tradeoff between fidelity to the original font, and efficient storage. This is an open problem.

To detect corners, we set a threshold at the 99 percentile of the cornerness array $c(x,y)$. We then locate points along the contours in Γ which are local maxima in $c(x,y)$ above the threshold, within a neighborhood of radius 4σ. This way the contours from an image such as the Kanizsa triangle illusion can be split into segments for separate smoothing (see figure 3.8).

We identify the straight parts of T-junctions by fitting three circular arcs at each triple point. Each uses points along one of the three paths passing through the triple point. The occluding contour is the one with the best fit whose error value falls below a maximum

Figure 3.5: The result of growing contours a distance of 4 by reflection at the endpoints in a line perpendicular to the edge direction near the endpoint. Compare this to figure 3.1. The growth points are retained only if growing the contour results in closure or connects it to another contour.

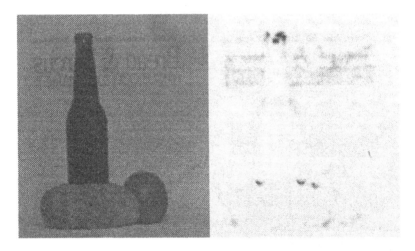

Figure 3.6: The cornerness measure of the still life picture. All corners and junctions have a strong response; texture also yields strong responses.

acceptable error. Our experiments all used a threshold of 2 pixel units, and 2σ points along each contour from the triple point. Because of shadows and shading, the problem of interpreting T-junctions locally is subtle, and will be discussed further in the next chapter.

We base our curve smoothing algorithm on the same procedure for finding the best fit to a circle or line used to interpret T-junctions.

3.3 Curve smoothing

We want a way of finding the circle or line that best fits a set of points $\{\mathbf{x}_i = (x_i, y_i), i = 1 \ldots n\}$ with weights w_i to indicate which points should be followed more closely, which less. We begin by looking at the square error, given a candidate center $\mathbf{c}$ and radius r, that is the weighted sum of radial distance squared from the circle to each point

$$\sum_i w_i(\|\mathbf{x}_i - \mathbf{c}\| - r)^2. \tag{3.1}$$

Assuming the $\mathbf{x}_i$ are all close to the candidate circle, we can use the approximation

$$\begin{aligned}
\sum_i w_i(\|\mathbf{x}_i - \mathbf{c}\|^2 - r^2)^2 &= \sum_i w_i(\|\mathbf{x}_i - \mathbf{c}\| + r)^2(\|\mathbf{x}_i - \mathbf{c}\| - r)^2 \\
&\cong (2r)^2 \sum_i w_i(\|\mathbf{x}_i - \mathbf{c}\| - r)^2.
\end{aligned}$$

We want to find $\mathbf{c}$ and r that minimize the approximation to 3.1

$$\sum_i w_i \frac{(\|x_i - \mathbf{c}\|^2 - r^2)^2}{4r^2}, \tag{3.2}$$

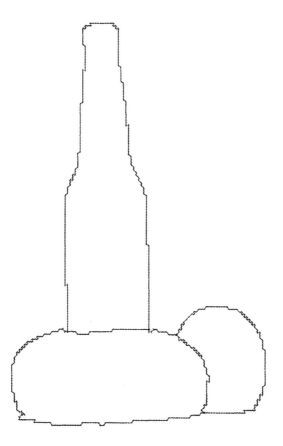

Figure 3.7: The result of deleting crack tips and closed contours less than 45 pixels. Compare to figure 3.5.

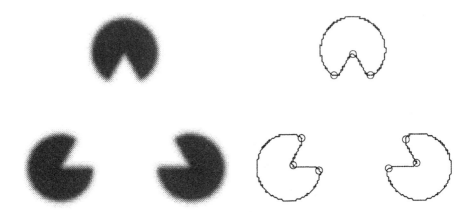

Figure 3.8: The Kanizsa triangle illusion, stored as a slightly blurred image rather than a geometric description file. Contour tracing first yields closed contours; these are split at the detected corners, marked by circles on the right hand picture.

but when $r \to \infty$ we want instead to construct the corresponding straight line. Writing the circle or line as $a + bx + cy + d(x^2 + y^2) = 0$, we seek the a, b, c and d that minimize

$$\frac{\sum_i w_i(a + bx_i + cy_i + d(x_i^2 + y_i^2))^2}{b^2 + c^2 - 4ad}.$$

To see that this approximates the best weighted fit, we can complete the squares to obtain

$$\sum_i w_i \frac{(\|x_i - \mathbf{c}\|^2 - r^2)^2}{4r^2}$$

$$\cong \frac{\sum_i w_i \left((x_i + \frac{b}{2d})^2 + (y_i + \frac{c}{2d})^2 + \frac{b^2 + c^2 - 4ad}{4d^2}\right)^2 d^2}{b^2 + c^2 - 4ad},$$

where $\mathbf{c} = (-b/2d, -c/2d)$ and $r = \sqrt{\frac{4ad + b^2 + c^2}{4d^2}}$.

The following algorithm constructs the best fitting circle or line to a weighted set of points. Form the $n \times 4$ matrix A

$$
\begin{aligned}
A_{i1} &= 1 \\
A_{i2} &= x_i \\
A_{i3} &= y_i \\
A_{i4} &= \|x_i\|^2.
\end{aligned}
$$

Fill a $1 \times n$ column vector W with weights for the x_i. Then seek a 4-vector $\mathbf{x} = (a\ b\ c\ d)$ that minimizes

$$\frac{{}^t\mathbf{x} \cdot {}^tA \cdot W \cdot A \cdot \mathbf{x}}{b^2 + c^2 - 4ad}.$$

This is done as follows.

1. Diagonalize the 4×4 symmetric matrix ${}^t A \cdot W \cdot A$ with an orthogonal matrix O_1:

$$ {}^t A \cdot W \cdot A = {}^t O_1 D_1 O_1 . $$

2. Let $\sqrt{D_1}$ be the diagonal matrix with the square roots of the elements of D_1, and $\sqrt{D_1}^{-1}$ the matrix with the inverse square roots of elements of D_1. If any element of D_1 is zero at this point, then there has been an exact fit of all points, and the algorithm yields $(a \ b \ c \ d) = {}^t(i\text{th column of } O_1)$.

Let

$$ A_2 = {}^t O_1 \cdot \sqrt{D_1} \cdot O_1 $$

and

$$ A_2^{-1} = {}^t O_1 \cdot \sqrt{D_1}^{-1} \cdot O_1 . $$

Note that A_2 and A_2^{-1} are symmetric positive definite, and $A_2^2 = {}^t A \cdot W \cdot A$.

3. Let

$$ E_1 = \begin{pmatrix} 0 & 0 & 0 & -2 \\ 0 & 1 & 0 & 0 \\ 0 & 0 & 1 & 0 \\ -2 & 0 & 0 & 0 \end{pmatrix} $$

be the matrix of $b^2 + c^2 - 4ad$, and let $E_2 = A_2^{-1} \cdot E_1 \cdot A_2^{-1}$. Note that E_2 is symmetric.

4. Finally, diagonalize E_2 with an orthogonal matrix O_2:

$$ E_2 = {}^t O_2 \cdot D_2 \cdot O_2 . $$

D_2 has three positive entries and one negative entry. Let λ_i be the largest positive entry. Then

$$ \mathbf{x} = (a \ b \ c \ d) = A_2^{-1} \cdot (i\text{th column of } O_2). $$

5. The error term in distance units is given by

$$ \frac{1}{\sqrt{\lambda_i / (\text{sum of weights in } W)}} . $$

This gives the best fitting circle

$$ a + bx + cy + d(x^2 + y^2) = 0. $$

If $|d|$ is very small (e.g., $< 10^{-15}$), then the $\mathbf{x}_i$ are considered best-fit by the line $a + bx + cy = 0$. Otherwise, they are best-fit by the circle with center $\mathbf{c} = (-b/(2d), -c/(2d))$ and radius $r = -a/d + \|\mathbf{c}\|^2$.

Figure 3.9 shows sample best-fits, using a staircase with constant weights $W = (1 \ 1 \cdots 1)$, and with Gaussian weights. The former yields a circle of noticeable radius

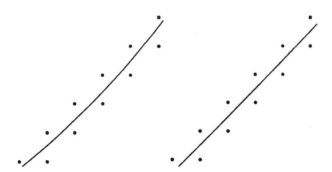

Figure 3.9: The best-fitting circle to a set of points in the form of a staircase $\{(0,0),(1,0),(1,1),\ldots,(5,5)\}$ with even weights, and with weights given by a Gaussian curve of standard deviation 2.5 centered over the middle point.

because of the relative skew of the two parallel rows of points. With Gaussian weights, the problem is effectively solved.

The curve-smoothing algorithm.

The curve smoothing algorithm based on this fitting function is as follows. Fix a standard deviation σ for the Gaussian weighting function (not the σ from the edge-finding algorithm), and fix an odd integer window size m, the number of points to fit at a time. Our implementation takes $m = \lfloor 4\sigma + 0.5 \rfloor + (1 - \lfloor 4\sigma + 0.5 \rfloor (\bmod 2))$.

The algorithm takes a list of n points $\{(x_i, y_i), i = 1 \ldots n\}$, and produces a refined list $\{(x'_i, y'_i, \theta_i, \kappa_i), i = 1 \ldots n\}$.

Build an array of one more than twice the window size $w_i, i = 1 \ldots 2m+1$ of weights given by
$$w_i = e^{-(i-m-1)^2/\sigma^2},$$
so that w_{m+1} is the peak of the sampled weighting function. The long tails of the weighting function let us assign the heaviest weight w_{m+1} to any point in a contour, even the endpoints, and still have enough weights on either side to fill the window size m.

It is important to understand that although the fitting algorithm finds a best-fit circle to a set of points, it will not be used to reduce the number of points in the representation of a contour. With each fit, we will update only one point–the one weighted the strongest–and use the best-fit circle for tangent and curvature estimates for the updated point.

This gives us a simple algorithm for smoothing a contour that is represented as a list of points. For each $i = 1, \ldots, n$, compute the best-fit to a circle or line of the point (x_i, y_i) and $m - 1$ of its neighbors as follows:

1. Define
$$\begin{aligned} l &= \max\{1, i - (m-1)/2\} \\ r &= \min\{l + m - 1, n\} \\ l_w &= m + 1 - (i - l), \text{ and} \\ r_w &= m + 1 + (r - i). \end{aligned}$$

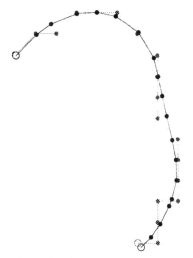

Figure 3.10: The curve smoothing algorithm applied to a contour from the contour tracing algorithm with $\sigma = 2.5$ and $m = 10$. The original curve is shown by a segmented line, the refined one by a solid line.

> These are the left and rightmost point indices and the left and rightmost weight indices respectively. This gives a window on the weight function such that the peak corresponds to the point (x_i, y_i) in the set of m points.

2. Use the algorithm described above to find the circle or line that best fits the points $(x_l, y_l), \ldots, (x_r, y_r)$ using the weights $w_{l_w}, \ldots, w_{r_w}$.

3. If the best-fit is a line, let (x_i', y_i') be the point on the line nearest (x_i, y_i); that is, the intersection of the best-fit line with a perpendicular line that goes through (x_i, y_i). Let θ_i be the tangent angle and $\kappa_i = 0$.

4. Otherwise, let (x_i', y_i') be the point on the best-fit circle nearest (x_i, y_i); that is, the point on the circle where it intersects the line from the center of the circle to (x_i, y_i). Let θ_i be the tangent to the circle at (x_i', y_i'), and let $\kappa_i = 1/r$ where r is the radius of the circle.

Thus we obtain refined locations, tangents, and curvatures for the points along a grid-sampled curve. Figure 3.10 shows the result of this algorithm applied to a point list produced by the curve tracing algorithm.

When treating a complete image, the endpoints of contours may be displaced slightly from the other contours to which they were attached. Our smoothing algorithm rejoins the junctions by intersecting line segments at corners and T-junctions, and computing the mean location of the three or four endpoints at other junctions. The result of applying this smoothing algorithm to the contours of figure 3.5 is shown in figure 3.11. Note that the contours that comprise the image boundary are not smoothed.

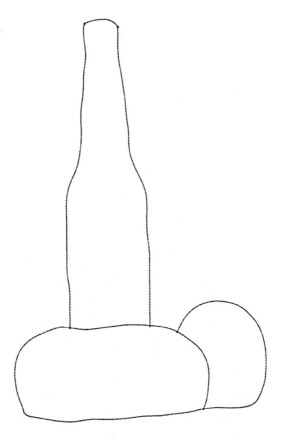

Figure 3.11: The result of smoothing the curves using the best fit to circle or line algorithm described, with $\sigma = 5$ and $m = 20$. The four junctions were interpreted as T-junctions as described, so that the "occluding" contours could be smoothed across each junction.

This final result is passed to the next stage of the algorithm as a set of contours, each represented as a list of point locations with tangent direction and curvature. Junctions are represented implicitly where contours end at exactly the same locations.

Chapter 4

Continuations

This chapter is about lines that *are not there* in the picture, but that really *are* there in the early stages of human visual perception.

Nearly every waking instant, the retina is exposed to the contours in two dimensions that come from projections of object boundaries in three dimensions. Consequently, one might argue that the brain learns which curves are more likely to occur as the outlines of 3D objects, and adapts according to one's surroundings. We can try to model this mathematically with a prior on the space of all curves, that is, a measure of likelihood on all possible curves which gives a higher number for curves that we are more likely to see. Of course the prior would change dependant upon the world in which the observer lived. Indoor scenes are composed primarily of straight lines and large flat surfaces, while in the rain forest there is rarely a straight line, and most surfaces have rich textures. Assuming the brain prefers short contours that are not too wiggly, we can construct a statistical prior based on the idea of elastica. The prior can then be used both to decide where a contour which disappears behind an occluding object is likely to reappear, and to compare two potential continuations for a given disrupted contour. David Mumford has worked out some of the details of elastica and priors on curves for vision in [26].

4.1 The psychology of continuations

We are interested in two questions: 1) How does the brain "fill in the gaps," and 2) What principles of organization drive the interpretation of overlapping objects? Following are several results in psychology research which address these questions.

Aligned terminators are a cue to occlusion.

The laboratory of von der Heydt [15] has found orientation-selective cells in area V2 of the the Macaque monkey that respond to the perceived boundaries formed by aligned terminators. These cells normally respond to dark lines or light/dark boundaries in a specific orientation; but in the experiment they responded to the subjective horizontal lines in the stimulus (see figure 4.1). Nakayama, Shimojo, and Paradiso [31, 36] have gone further to find that such contours elicit orientation–specific adaptation with tuning characteristics comparable to real contours. Nakayama and Shimojo [32] make a convincing argument

Figure 4.1: Aligned terminators are a strong cue to occlusion. Heydt et al found cells that responded to the horizontal bar and the illusory contours but not the vertical grating lines.

that occlusion contours must be recognized as such very early in the visual organizing process.

Both amodal and modal continuations are the result of the same early visual process.

Visible contours are called *modal*; occluded contours are called *amodal*. The same distinction applies to continuations: modal continuations are accompanied by a perceived difference in brightness across them, although there is no difference in the reflected light, such as with the sides of the white triangle in Kanizsa's triangle illusion (figure 1.5). The arcs that make the black pac-man shapes seem like occluded circles are amodal continuations.

Kellman and Shipley conjecture [18] that the brain fills in gaps the same way, that is, following the same rules, irrespective of whether a continuation is modal or amodal. As evidence they use a figure similar to figure 4.2. At first glance, one tends to see one amorphous blob occluding the other, with a slight difference in blackness across the modally completed lines. However, either surface can be interpreted as nearer, bringing the difference in blackness effect with it.

One can use an effect called *neon color-spreading* to make more explicit the shapes of modally-completed contours. For example, in one diagram a black circle "occludes" a red X, with only the tips of the X peeking out from behind the black circle. When stereopsis is used to bring the bits of the occluded X nearer in depth than the black circle, one perceives very strongly a translucent red X atop the black circle. The effect occurs at a perceptual level that makes it difficult to examine the continuations carefully, so in the case of the red X, it is not clear whether the perceived continuations actually form corners. However, the phenomenon of neon color spreading can be used to show that a partly hidden corner of a square does not necessarily complete into a square. The missing corner may instead be completed by a rounded contour. This supports a theory of continuations based on local properties of curves rather than higher-level preferences for "square" shapes.

Completions do not necessarily make sense.

Kanizsa's experiments [17] show that people often make interpolations automatically and without thinking whether the organization of surfaces is justified by the visible parts of a

Figure 4.2: A shape that produces both occluded contour continuations and amodal contours. After fixing on it for half a minute or less, the figure and ground appear to reverse, with no change in the two perceived shapes.

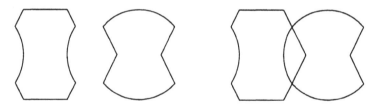

Figure 4.3: When joined, the two shapes on the left form a figure of two overlapped, nonsymmetric shapes. From Kanizsa.

scene. For instance, subjects may report "seeing" partly occluded objects, contradicting facts one knows about the shapes and sizes of common objects (see figure 1.2, from [17] p. 41).

Kanizsa has also made a strong case against the gestaltist principles of maximal symmetry and maximal simplicity. Figure 4.3 shows that neither principle drives the interpretation of the whole figure. Instead, one sees convex, overlapping figures whose boundaries do not have corners. Kanizsa concludes that that convexity prevails over symmetry (see also figure 4.4). It is clear also that where four contours meet at a point, the straighter continuations prevail. This idea is so basic that one does not imagine that it might not be true.

Figure 1.2 suggests a further principle which the 2.1-D sketch functional does not capture. When two sets of continuations are pitted against each other, like the man's pants and the fence, the shorter ones complete modally and the longer ones amodally. Figure

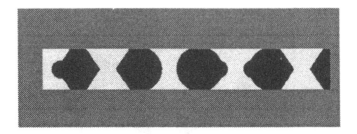

Figure 4.4: Convexity prevails over symmetry. We perceive the convex shapes as figure, and the symmetric shapes as ground. From Kanizsa.

Figure 4.5: Shorter continuations tend to be modal, while the longer ones tend to be amodal; hence the bulges appear to occlude the tails. From Kanizsa.

4.5 also illustrates the effect.

T-junctions compete with other occlusion cues such as stereopsis.

Figure 4.6 shows a cross pattern consisting of a horizontal bar of one color and two short vertical segments of another color. Viewed with binocular disparity cues that put the vertical bars in front, one tends still to perceive a single vertical bar behind the horizontal bar, in spite of the depth cue from stereo.

Stereopsis is known to be a weak cue for depth recovery in general. When a face mask is viewed from the inside, we tend to perceive an ordinary face, that is, inverted with respect to the depth information from stereopsis, particularly when the lighting comes from below. One reason for this may be that all the shape information comes from shading rather than sharpness of features such as lines and corners. The extremely familiar shape of faces may also make the depth-reversal difficult to perceive. This effect may be due to the weakness of shading as a depth cue or to the importance of familiarity in interpreting surface shape.

Other experiments have shown that stereopsis can win out over T-junctions, and motion cues can be stronger than both stereopsis and T-junctions. The important point is that T-junctions are among the sometimes competing sources of occlusion information in vision.

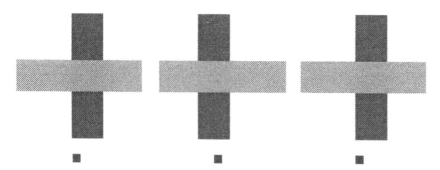

Figure 4.6: Competing occlusion cues: a horizontal bar in front of a vertical bar by pictorial cues. Binocular disparity puts the vertical bar in front. Nearly all viewers perceive the horizontal bar in front. Crossed fusers should fuse the center and right images; uncrossed fusers should fuse the center and left images.

Grouping for recognition comes after occlusion labeling of edges.

Nakayama and Shimojo ran a novel experiment to show how relative depths across edges are used in the early stages of visual processing to group together parts of a partly covered object [32]. Subjects were visually trained on several faces so that they could recognize and distinguish them. Then the test group was shown partly covered faces selected at random. Stereopsis was used to bring the uncovered parts of the face either nearer or farther than the horizontal bands of noise, as illustrated in figure 4.7. Naïve subjects reported in all cases that the faces were easier to recognize when the horizontal bands of noise were nearer rather than farther than the horizontal strips of the face. This was supported by a greater accuracy in the recognition task.

The authors argue that this comes from an early labeling of edge "ownership" or "belongingness." When the horizontal noise stripes are nearer, the edges they share with the alternating horizontal face stripes "belong" to the closer noise stripes. This lets the farther face information continue behind the occluders. When instead the face stripes are nearer, the edges belong to the face stripes which then become complete shapes in themselves and are not grouped together or continued. The experiment bears on the present work in that it shows that stereopsis can slow down or interfere with completions from T-junctions.

All of this suggests that human interpolations are not fully predictable, and may yet involve constructions based on a complex set of remembered shapes. However, it seems that some of the essential early perceptual "rules" can be captured in a simple form. The next section studies one possible such form, a family of energy-minimizing curves that comes from $E_{2.1}$.

4.2 Elastica

Recall that the 2.1-D sketch model describes an image by a set of shapes $R_i, i = 1 \dots n$, ordered by occlusion, so that $R_1 < R_2 < \dots < R_n = D$. Suppose a region R_i disappears

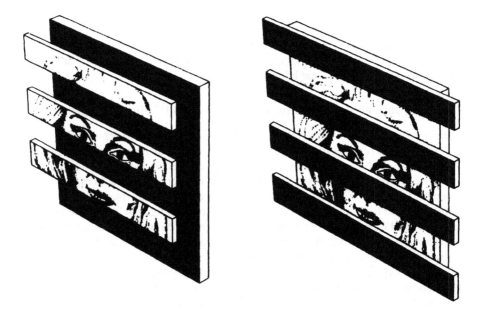

Figure 4.7: An illustration of the two stimuli used in Nakayama and Shimojo's occlusion experiment. In one case, horizontal bands of noise are the nearer occluders, with strips of the face visible between them. In the other case, the strips of face are the nearer occluders. Both stimuli contain the same face information; in fact the only difference comes from stereo disparity of the bands of noise.

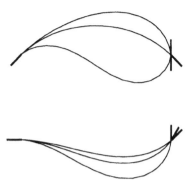

Figure 4.8: Several elastica with fixed endpoints and end tangents.

behind occluding objects at $P_0 \in \partial R_i$ and reappears at P_1. Let t_0 and t_1 be the unit tangent vectors to ∂R_i at P_0 and P_1. Then we can characterize the invisible portion Γ of ∂R_i between P_0 and P_1 as the curve which minimizes:

$$\int_\Gamma (\nu + \alpha\kappa^2)ds$$

subject to the boundary conditions of beginning at (P_0, t_0) and ending at (P_1, t_1).

This particular variational problem has a long history, having been first investigated by Euler in 1744[1]. Curves that minimize this integral have been called "elastica" since then, and have appeared here and there, especially in treatises on elasticity (cf. [21], Chapter 19 and [4] for a recent treatment). One reason why they are not better known is that they are not expressible by simple functions, but require elliptic or similar functions.

Putting complex coordinates in the plane, they may, for instance, be written as logarithmic derivatives of the theta function:

$$F(z) = \frac{\partial}{\partial z} log\theta(\omega, x + a) - b \cdot x$$

where

$$\theta(\omega, x) = \sum_n e^{\pi i n^2 \omega + 2\pi i n x}$$

and either

$$\omega = it, \quad a = \tfrac{it}{2}, \quad b = F'(\tfrac{1}{2} - \tfrac{it}{4}), \quad \text{some real } t, \text{ or}$$

$$\omega = \tfrac{it+1}{2}, \quad a = 0, \quad b = F'(\tfrac{1}{4} + \tfrac{it}{4}), \quad \text{some real } t.$$

These forms generate the minimizing curves for any ν and α including those that make loops, i.e. which are minima in the topological class of curves with each possible total turning angle between P_0 and P_1. Some examples are shown in figure 4.8.

Computationally, the simplest way to solve for them seems to be hill-climbing: start with a convenient chain $P_0 = x_0, x_1, \ldots, x_N = P_1$ of points joining P_0 and P_1 for which

---

[1]*De Curvis Elastica*, an appendix to [8].

$x_1 - x_0 = constant \cdot t_0$ and $x_{N-1} - x_N = constant \cdot t_1$ and let it evolve to decrease $\int (\nu + \alpha\kappa^2)ds$. Thus we may estimate the curvature κ_i at x_i as:

$$\kappa_i = \frac{\theta_i - \theta_{i-1}}{(d_i + d_{i-1})/2}$$

where $x_{i+1} - x_i$ has length d_i and orientation θ_i. Its second derivative can be estimated by:

$$\kappa_i^{**} = \frac{2\kappa_{i+1}}{d_i(d_i + d_{i-1})} - \frac{2\kappa_i}{d_i d_{i-1}} + \frac{2\kappa_{i-1}}{d_{i-1}(d_i + d_{i-1})}$$

Then the curve evolves by:

$$\text{new } x_i = x_i + \epsilon(\nu\kappa_i + \alpha\kappa_i^3 - 2\alpha\kappa_i^{**}) \cdot (-sin(\theta_i), cos(\theta_i)),$$

for $2 \le i \le N - 2$ (n.b. x_0, x_1, x_{N-1} and x_N stay fixed).

The derivation is given in Mumford [26].

4.3   Matching ends and computing continuations

Recall that at this point the algorithm has extracted a set of contours $\Gamma = \{\gamma_1, \ldots, \gamma_h\}$ which meet each other only at their endpoints.

This second stage aims to find complete configurations of contours, each of which is made up of the curves in Γ together with some continuations that connect compatible pairs of endpoints in Γ. The ideal is of course to link up endpoints of curves that are part of the same object outline. Recall however that we assume no cognitive recognition using a priori knowledge of specific shapes. The algorithm must depend on little more than a statistical prior that prefers short contours that are not too wiggly.

The most simple-minded way to match up pairs of endpoints would be to build continuations connecting every pair of distinct endpoints, and then select from these consistent subsets that yield the lowest penalties from the contour term of $E_{2.1}$.

If Γ has h contours, then there are $2h$ endpoints, so that with no restrictions there would be $4h^2 - 2h$ possible continuations, and an absurd $2^{8h^3(h-1)+h}$ possible complete configurations. We can evaluate a configuration by adding the contour penalties of continuations to the angle penalties of corners and junctions which are not completed, so in principle we can find the best configurations. In practice we have to pare down the astronomical number of possibilities. Fortunately there are simple heuristics to disqualify certain pairs of endpoints as incompatible.

A first heuristic requires that the length of a continuation not exceed five times the length of either of the contours it would join. Thus, if two curves of length 1 are 5 units apart, the continuation connecting them is disqualified. In some cases this disqualifies a good match, such as in figure 4.9. The implementation takes as a parameter this ratio of contour to continuation length.

A second heuristic concerns the average intensities (or eventually colors) on either sides of paired T-junctions. It requires that either (a) the color of at least one side of one T roughly match the corresponding side of the other, or (b) that the light/dark relationship

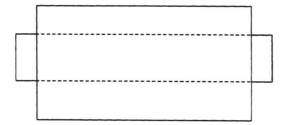

Figure 4.9: The continuations, shown as dashed lines, are more than five times longer than either of their visible segments.

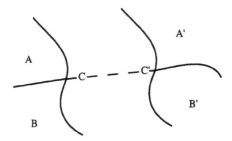

Figure 4.10: Two T-junctions to be matched. A, B, A', and B' are averaged brightness (or color) using an oblong Gaussian weighting function aligned with the tangents at the contour endpoints.

of the sides of one T be respected by the sides of the other. Referring to figure 4.10, we write this as

$$|A - A'| < \delta, \text{ or}$$
$$|B - B'| < \delta, \text{ or}$$
$$\text{if } |A - A'| > \delta \text{ and } |B - B'| > \delta, \text{ then } A < B \text{ as } A' < B',$$

for some δ. The implementation uses $\delta = 0.1(I_{max} - I_{min})$.

A third heuristic asks that the complete configuration be consistent as it is being built up. Thus, if one of the three contours meeting at a triple-point is continued, that is, the triple-point is interpreted as a T-junction with that one contour as the disrupted one, this imposes an order relation on the three regions separated by the triple-point. In figure 4.10, adding the dashed continuation would impose $C < A$, $C < B$, $C' < A'$, $C' < B'$, where $<$ means nearer to the viewer.

Williams has developed a method of occlusion labeling somewhat akin to this approach [42]. His method is to assign to each contour either an occlusion orientation (i.e., to label one side of the contour as belonging to the nearer surface), or a value meaning "no occlusion." He then expresses constraints as inequalities using this three-value system, and performs constraint relaxation via an integer linear program to find an optimal plausible labeling for all edges and corners. Several perceptual rules of thumb are built into his integer constraints:

1. Bring whole objects forward;

2. Prefer convex corners over concave corners in objects;

3. Prefer straight continuations over corners in objects; and

4. Bring forward objects with closely-spaced parallel outlines.

The 2.1-D sketch model indirectly enforces the second and third of these, but not the fourth, although it is indeed important–consider the branches of a tree–and worthy of incorporation into more complete refinement of our model. Williams's model does not go so far as to find a complete description of a scene in terms of overlapping shapes; this has the advantage of correctly labeling contours in scenes with interwoven or self-overlapping surfaces.

Using splines for elastica

The algorithm searches over all consistent sets of continuations, remembering the ten best at any time. To speed estimates, rather than compute the elastica for a continuation, we compute the third order spline $s(t) = (x(t), y(t))$ which minimizes the sum of length and curvature squared. Given two endpoints $(x(0), y(0))$ and $(x(1), y(1))$ and tangents $(x'(0), y'(0))$ and $(x'(1), y'(1))$, we compute the spline connecting them as

$$
\begin{aligned}
x(t) &= a + bt + ct^2 + dt^3 \\
a &= x(0) \\
b &= \eta x'(0) \\
c &= 3(x(1) - x(0)) - \eta(2x'(0) + x'(1)) \\
d &= 2(x(0) - x(1)) + \eta(x'(0) + x'(1))
\end{aligned}
$$

$$
\begin{aligned}
y(t) &= e + ft + gt^2 + ht^3 \\
e &= y(0) \\
f &= \eta y'(0) \\
g &= 3(y(1) - y(0)) - \eta(2y'(0) + y'(1)) \\
h &= 2(y(0) - y(1)) + \eta(y'(0) + y'(1))
\end{aligned}
$$

where η is the "speed" of the spline at both $t = 0$ and $t = 1$, which we vary to minimize the integral $\int_{t=0}^{1} (\nu + \alpha \kappa^2) ds$, with

$$
\kappa = \frac{x'(t)y''(t) - y'(t)x''(t)}{(x'^2(t) + y'^2(t))^{(3/2)}}
$$

and $ds = \sqrt{x'^2(t) + y'^2(t)} dt$. This spline is emphatically not the same as an elastica; however, it can be computed in about 1/100,000th the time. Figure 4.11 compares the two energy-minimizing curves for one choice of endpoints and tangents. To create the spline in this picture, we actually varied the speeds at both $t = 0$ and $t = 1$ independently. The spline is still notably different from the elastica. This illustrates that the class of splines is a very small subset of the vastly larger class of smooth curves with given endpoints and tangents. (See figure 4.11).

Figure 4.11: A spline that minimizes a sum of length and curvature squared, shown as a solid line, together with an elastica, i.e., a smooth curve that minimizes the same functional, shown as a dashed line. In both cases, $\nu = 0.5, \alpha = 0.1$.

The penalty measure of a set of continuations is the sum of the length and curvature terms from $E_{2.1}$ over all contours including the proposed continuation splines, plus the angle penalties of all corners which are not continued, and angle penalties of both corners at each T which is not continued. Thus an unmatched T is worse than an unmatched corner.

Recursive search

The actual search works as follows. One data structure holds the current set of possible continuations to be added; this is passed down the recursion so each level has its own idea of what continuations are allowed. The recursive function is defined by:

- An end condition: If there are no further continuations allowed in the current state, then compute the penalty for the current set of continuations and store if in the top ten.

- Recursion with no added continuations: Choose one possible continuation. Delete it from the current state *without* adding it to the current set of continuations and recurse.

- Recursion with one added continuation: Choose one possible continuation. Add it to the current set of continuations, propogate the constraints it imposes on the current state, and recurse. Suppose the continuation connects $\gamma_a(0)$ to $\gamma_b(0)$. The constraints first disqualify (a) any continuation of either $\gamma_a(0)$ or $\gamma_b(0)$ to any other points. Then, if the continuation was the fourth contour meeting at endpoint $\gamma_a(0)$ (and/or $\gamma_b(0)$), there are two other disqualifications: (b) any continuations ending at $\gamma_a(0)$ (and/or $\gamma_b(0)$); and (c) any continuations that would defy the order relations dictated by the interpretation of the T-junction at $\gamma_a(0)$ (and/or $\gamma_b(0)$).

4.4   Results

When processing the still life in 3.11, the algorithm disqualifies, of 112 possible endpoint pairings, 33 due to length, and 30 due to unmatched intensities. Of the remaining

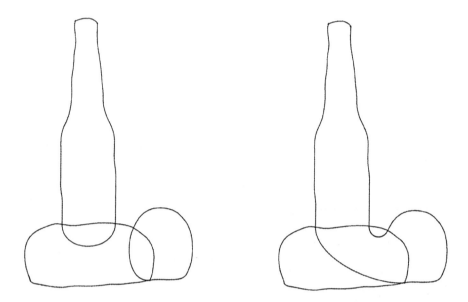

Figure 4.12: The best and second-best sets of continuations for the still life found by the algorithm. $\nu = .1, \alpha = \beta = 10$.

configurations, 36 are disqualified by ordering relations. Runtime to find the top ten configurations for the still life is approximately 10 seconds on a Sparcstation I.

The best set of continuations completes the bottle and the nectarine as we would expect; the second best actually completes the bottle and nectarine together, as shown in figure 4.12.

The Kanizsa triangle illusion (figure 3.8) requires stricter angle and curvature penalties to force the relatively long continuations that create the triangle. The best set of continuations corresponds to our interpretation, shown in figure 4.13. The lines are not straight because the edge detection stage did not yield straight lines. The processing time for this figure was three times longer than for the still life; this is because the algorithm does not try to interpret ordering relations implied by continuations of corners as it does for T-junctions.

Delaying the interpretation of T-junctions

Even with a careful choice of scale, we cannot depend on the interpretation of T-junctions from a best-fit on pairs of contours near the junction. As we have seen in the still life, the lower-rightmost junction is misleading because the bottom of the potato nearly aligns with the bottom of the nectarine; and the shadow obscures the subtle cue that would make a correct interpretation possible. It is also common that an occluding object casts a shadow on a farther object just near the occlusion, so that T-junctions detected by gradient alone

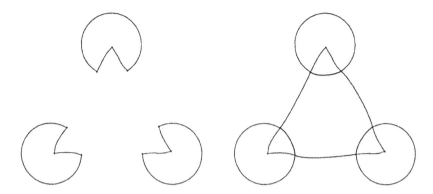

Figure 4.13: Contours from Kanizsa's triangle diagram, with continuations found by the algorithm; $\nu = 1, \alpha = 100, \beta = 200$.

cannot be correctly interpreted. Many of the junctions in figure 4.15 mislead the best-fit interpretation (see the raw edge output in figure 4.16). Because of these problems, we designed the continuation stage of our algorithm to search over a larger space of possible continuations, interpreting T-junctions in all sensible ways.

We can simply delay the interpretation of T-junctions altogether until after a suitable set of continuations has been chosen; then treat the two contours at each T that are *not* continued as part of a single contour, and re-smooth the contours accordingly. The result is somewhat more pleasing to the eye (see figure 4.14).

Initial smoothing of contours is still needed to estimate edge tangent and curvature for the later stages. It smooths sections of contours separately without interpreting T-junctions. Junctions are rejoined by averaging the positions of the three endpoints to form a new junction point. The resulting jogs in the contours will be eliminated during the second smoothing stage (see figures 4.17 and 4.20), and do not effect the construction of continuations.

Final output

The third stage of the 2.1-D sketch algorithm needs the area and average luminance of each region, several quantities concerning each contour including the continuations, and information about the configuration of contours and regions in the image. These data are straightforward to extract. To label regions we fill an array of the same size as the input image with zeroes, except at contour points; then we use a four-connected flood fill to label noncontour pixels with region numbers, counting pixels and summing luminance values for each region. This yields an image with the region numbers at each noncontour pixel for building the oriented graph, with which it is easy to derive the region number on one's left as one travels along a contour γ_i in a given direction.

We now have a set of contours together with plausible continuations, contour lengths, and other associated quantities needed to find the 2.1-D sketch by minimizing $E_{2.1}$.

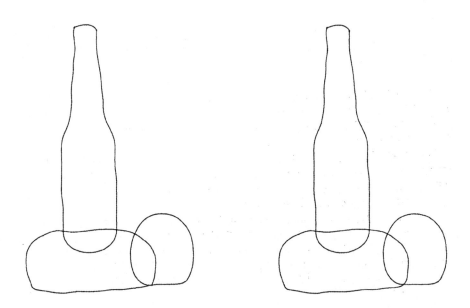

Figure 4.14: Left: completions as in figure 4.12. Right: same, with contours smoothed across the T-junctions which have been correctly interpreted based on which endpoints have been continued.

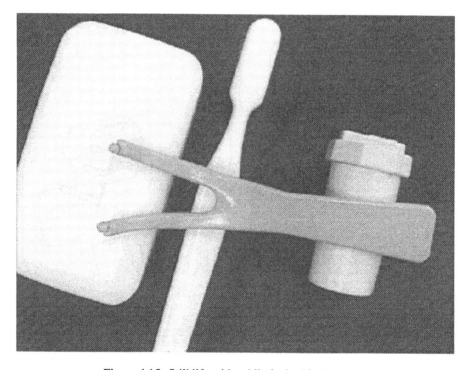

Figure 4.15: Still life with subliminal ad for bar soap.

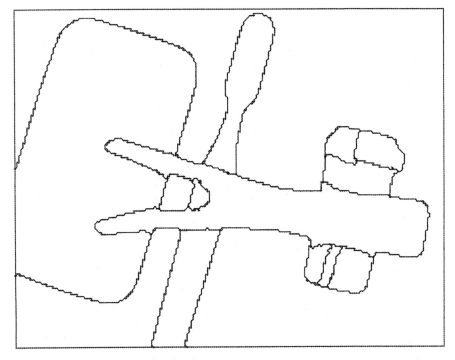

Figure 4.16: Toiletries output from the contour tracer with $\sigma = 1.25$, gap-jumping by up to 7 pixels, and cornerness threshold at the 99.9 percentile. Shadows give unexpected results at nearly all junctions.

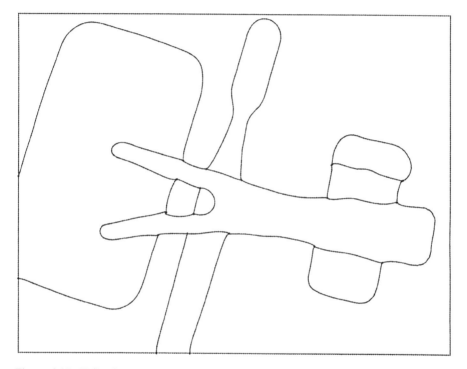

Figure 4.17: Toiletries contours smoothed without first interpreting junctions where $\sigma = 12$; $w = 24$. Three of the contours from shadows on the lens case have been removed by hand to reduce the number of regions for the final combinatoric stage. The abrupt jumps in position at junctions is only visually displeasing; tangent and curvature estimates remain consistent at the endpoints.

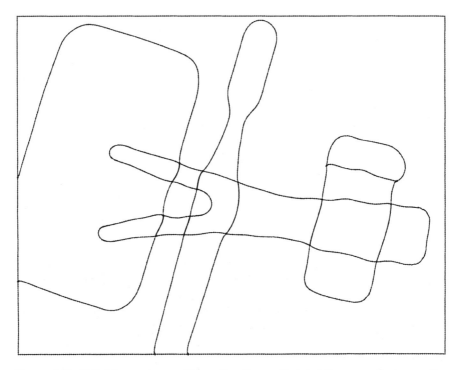

Figure 4.18: Toiletries contours with continuations added and then smoothed according to the interpretations of T-junctions dictated by the continuations where $\nu = .1, \alpha = \beta = 10, \sigma = 5$. Of 1740 possible continuations, 328 touched the boundary of the image, 348 were too long, and 235 were disqualified because the luminance values did not match near the endpoints. Running time was 130 minutes on a Sparcstation I+ searching over all continuations for each endpoint. Running time was reduced to 4 minutes using only the best 2 continuations for each endpoint.

Figure 4.19: Blades of grass.

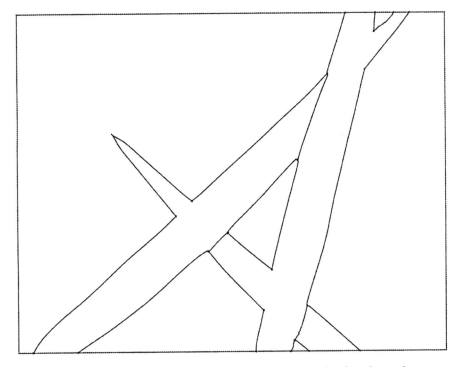

Figure 4.20: Grass contours smoothed without first interpreting junctions where $\sigma =$ 12, $w = 24$. Note that the edge detection stage failed to find three contours. Corner detection compensates using the 99.3 percentile of the cornerness measure.

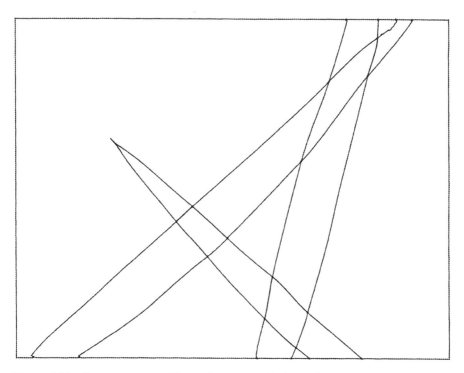

Figure 4.21: Grass contours with continuations added and then smoothed according to the interpretations of T-junctions dictated by the continuations where $\nu = .1, \alpha = \beta = 10, \sigma = 10$. Of 1740 possible continuations, 142 were too long, and 131 were disqualified because the luminance values did not match near the endpoints. Running time was 70 minutes on a Sparcstation I. Running time was reduced to 5 minutes using only the best two continuations for each endpoint.

Chapter 5

Finding the 2.1D Sketch

The third stage of the algorithm finds the 2.1D sketch of an image whose region boundaries lie along a set of prescribed edges. This chapter describes the basic algorithm and heuristic refinements, and shows results for the images shown in the previous chapters.

5.1 Recursive search

At this point we have $\Gamma = \{\gamma_1, \ldots, \gamma_g\}$, a set of non-self-intersecting contours which meet each other and ∂D only at endpoints. (In the figures, the γ_i correspond to the contours that connect junction to junction, corner to junction, and corner to corner; these include both visible contours and continuations.) We let $\Pi = \{P_1, \ldots, P_n\}$ be the closures of the connected components of $D\backslash\Gamma$. The algorithm must now solve the problem of finding an overlapping segmentation $(\{R_i\}, <)$ of D which minimizes $E_{2.1}$ such that $\partial R_i \subset \cup\Gamma$.

The input to the algorithm is a small set of scalar values from which we can derive an embedded oriented planar graph whose edges are the $\gamma \in \Gamma$. The graph is oriented arbitrarily. The values necessary, for each $\gamma \in \Gamma$ and for each $P \in \Pi$, are:

1. $|\gamma\backslash\partial D|$, the length of the contour;

2. $\int_{\gamma\backslash\partial D} \phi(\kappa)ds$, the curvature term of E computed on the contour except where it coincides with ∂D;

3. $\arg \dot{\gamma}(0)$ and $\arg \dot{\gamma}(1)$, the orientations of the tangents at the endpoints of the contour;

4. $\bar{g}_P$, the *mean* value of an image function $g : D \to \mathbf{R}$ on P; and

5. $|P|$, the area of P.

The vertices V of the embedded graph are the set of points in D which are endpoints of some γ. To specify the graph structure, it suffices to associate, to each contour γ,

6. $v_{0,\gamma}$ and $v_{1,\gamma}$, the vertices it links, and

7. $P_{0,\gamma}$ and $P_{1,\gamma}$, the faces it separates,

labeled so that as one travels from $v_{0,\gamma}$ to $v_{1,\gamma}$, $P_{0,\gamma}$ is on one's left and $P_{1,\gamma}$ on one's right.

Given this input, complete combinatoric search is most quickly achieved by computing optimal segmentations for all subsets of Π whose unions have connected interior, starting with just single regions P, then in groups of two, three, and so on, each time using the previous results.

First we calculate the energy of the trivial segmentation of each P as an image, that is, $E_P = \epsilon|P|$, as well as the boundary energy, for ∂P broken down into l lists $\{\gamma_1, \ldots, \gamma_{k_i}\}_{i=1}^l$, tracing each closed contour of the boundary of P. (P may have "holes" in it.) The boundary energy is

$$B_P = \sum_{i=1}^l \sum_{j=1}^{k_i} \int_{\gamma_j \backslash \partial D} \phi(\kappa)ds + \beta|\arg \dot{\gamma}_j(0) - \arg \dot{\gamma}_{j-1}(1)|,$$

where $\gamma_{-1} = \gamma_{k_i}$ to make the calculation trace the whole closed contour. The terms containing $\dot{\gamma}_j(x)$ are understood to be zero whenever $\gamma_j(x) \in \partial D$.

Note that to extract the lists $\gamma_1, \ldots, \gamma_{k_i}$ that trace the closed contours of ∂P, the algorithm requires items 3, 6, and 7 of the input. Also note that all the $\gamma_j(x)$ are reparameterized for P so that $\gamma_j(0) = \gamma_{j-1}(1)$.

Recall that Π contains n regions, say $P_1, \ldots, P_n$. Next we calculate the energy for pairs of regions whose union has connected interior using the B_P and E_P; and continue for triples and so on, so that for every $T \subset \Pi$ with fewer than n regions, and whose union has connected interior, $E_{\cup T}$ and $B_{\cup T}$ have been computed for the optimal segmentation of $\cup T$ considered as an image in its own right. We must also keep enough information to re-construct the optimal overlapping segmentation $(\{R_i\}, <)$ for any such T.

To segment all of D, we consider two subsets of Π: the regions belonging to the background, i.e., the furthest region, and those belonging to some other region. We will call these P and Q respectively. For every proper subset $Q \subset \Pi$, and for every subset $P \subset \Pi$ whose union is connected, and whose complement in D is contained in $\cup Q$, we compute the energy

$$E_D = E_P + \sum_{R \in C(Q)} E_R,$$

where $C(Q) = \{$ maximal subsets of Q whose unions have connected interior $\}$, E_P is the energy computed on the single region $\cup P$, and E_R is the energy of the optimally segmented $R \subset \Pi$ previously computed. The P and Q that achieve a minimum E_D give the optimal segmentation of D, which can be expressed recursively as $P <$ optimal-segmentation(Q).

In our implementation, then, the information stored with any T of i regions consists in two sets of regions, a set $T_{\text{background}}$ whose union has connected interior, and another set $T_{\text{foreground}}$ which has less than i regions, and may have more than one component of connected interior. The overlapping segmentation can be rebuilt by using the information already stored for each component of $T_{\text{foreground}}$.

This performs an exhaustive search, and finds the 2.1D sketch for the image, given the curves and continuations from the first two stages. The search takes exponential time in the number of regions n depending on the shape of the graph.

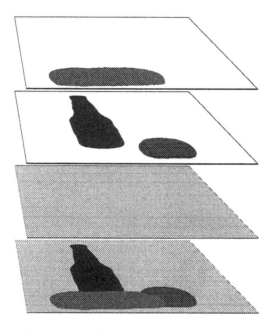

Figure 5.1: The 2.1D sketch of the still life using the optimal set of continuations; $\nu = 1, \alpha = 20, \beta = 30, \epsilon = .0049$.

5.2 Results on pictures

The two segmentations for the still life picture are shown in figures 5.1 and 5.2. These diagrams are the actual output of the segmentation stage in a printer language. The bottom layer is a piecewise constant segmentation without overlaps that assigns to each region its average intensity value. Then each layer going up from the bottom shows overlapping regions that are successively nearer the viewer. Each completed region is shown with a constant intensity which is the average of the visible parts of that region. Several disjoint shapes are shown at the same level although the 2.1D sketch has assigned arbitrary depth relations between them.

In figure 5.1, the background region is rearmost and is the entire image domain; next are the completed bottle and nectarine, and the potato is foremost, i.e., in front of everything else. Figure 5.2 came from the suboptimal set of continuations, and required an adjustment of parameters to force the bottle and nectarine be joined in spite of their difference in average brightness.

The Kanizsa triangle diagram with completions is correctly segmented into three black circles behind a nearer white triangle which is the same color as the background (figure 5.3). The sides of the triangle are only as straight as the original contours and continuations.

The grass image (figure 5.4). is also segmented in the correct way. Note that the center region is not brought forward but becomes part of the background. The absence of

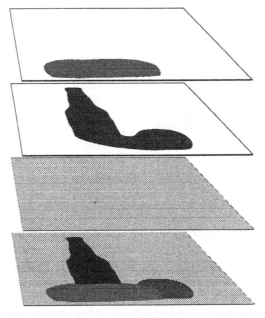

Figure 5.2: The 2.1D sketch of the still life using the suboptimal set of continuations; the bottle and nectarine are actually the same object, connected behind the potato. The curvature and corner penalties had to be increased to force the bottle and nectarine to be joined in spite of the difference in their average intensities; $\nu = .1, \alpha = 300, \beta = 2000, \epsilon = .0049$.

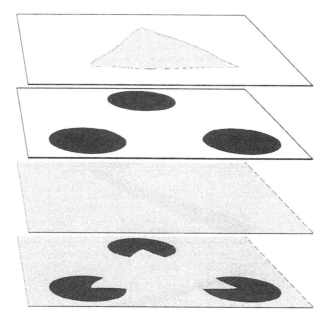

Figure 5.3: The 2.1D sketch of the Kanizsa triangle; $\nu = 1, \alpha = 1000, \beta = 1000, \epsilon = .0078$.

several line segments in the original contour image was compensated by the continuation stage, allowing the complete reconstruction of the 2.1D sketch. The sides of the triangle are only as straight as the original contours and continuations.

The final example of a correct segmentation is shown in figure 5.5. In this segmentation, the cap of the lens case on the right-hand side does not have a sufficiently distinct average brightness to merit the introduction of two corners, so it is merged with the lens case. The black region between the prongs of the fork is merged with the background.

Failures.

The following are several examples of pictures for which the 2.1D sketch algorithm *cannot* succeed.

- In scenes of geometric solids like furniture, buildings and walls, there are many non-occlusion edges where surface orientation changes abruptly, for example, where walls meet. Many junctions in these scenes do not have meaningful continuations. Figure 5.6 shows the incorrect set of continuations found by the algorithm for a blocks world image. The 2.1D sketch model is not designed to represent these scenes. Figure 5.7 shows a typical 2.1D sketch for a blocks world scene.

- Strong shadows can hide important object boundaries and junctions, such as in figure 5.8. Correct continuations depend on finding the structurally important junctions.

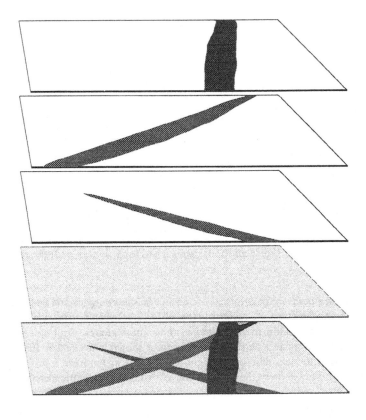

Figure 5.4: The 2.1D sketch of the grass image; $\nu = .1, \alpha = \beta = 10, \epsilon = .0078$. Running time was a hefty 420 minutes on a Sparcstation I.

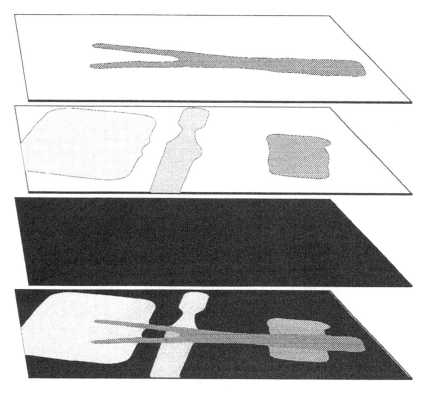

Figure 5.5: The 2.1D sketch of the toiletries; $\nu = .1, \alpha = \beta = 10, \epsilon = .0078$. Running time was approximately 250 minutes on a Sparcstation I.

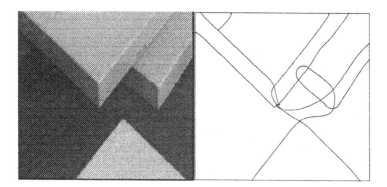

Figure 5.6: A blocks world image, segmented and with the optimal continuations added; $\nu = .1, \alpha = \beta = 10$. With $\nu = 100$, no continuations are added. The smoothed contours without continuations were used to find the 2.1D sketch shown in figure 5.7.

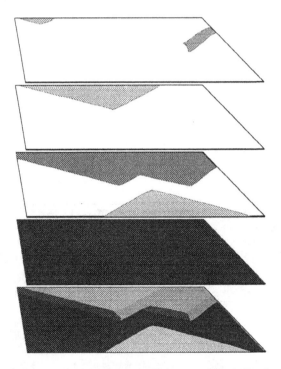

Figure 5.7: The 2.1D sketch of a blocks world image. The 2.1D sketch model is not designed to represent continuous surfaces with discontinuous surface normal.

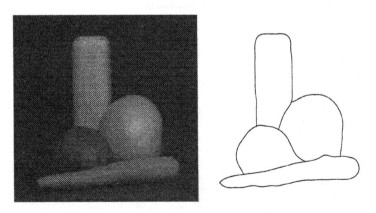

Figure 5.8: Still life with soy milk. The shadow hides a structurally important junction on the lower-right portion of the nectarine, making it difficult to find appropriate continuations.

- Self-overlapping regions, such as a garden hose, and interwoven surfaces, such as a weave, are not representable in the 2.1D sketch, because of the strict depth ordering of regions.

Chapter 6

Conclusion

We have taken a novel approach the computational task of image segmentation by incorporating occlusion detection at a low level.

This work offers a new data structure for early visual processing, the 2.1-D sketch, which captures the essential organization of surfaces in a scene that is missing from two-dimensional maps, without asking for a more detailed reconstruction of the third dimension. In Marr's program, algorithms for early visual processing were judged by how effectively their output could be used to estimate surface orientation and distance to viewer. This $2\frac{1}{2}$D sketch has been difficult to estimate, and moreover leaves unfinished the task of segmentation into regions or objects of interest. Our simpler sketch represents a scene as a group of overlapping shapes corresponding to the projections of objects. It gives both a segmentation into regions of interest and depth relations between surfaces, together with a first guess for the completions of occluded objects.

This first guess at completions is not in itself a novel contribution as it follows a long line of research on what constitutes a good continuation of a disrupted contour. However, this is the first instance where elastica, curves which minimize a sum of length and the square of curvature, appear in computer vision. What is truly novel is that our continuations fall out of a larger functional that defines a complete organization of surfaces in a scene. Resulting organizations include only consistent continuations, even if certain better continuations exist for particular disrupted contours considered in themselves.

Each stage of the algorithm that finds the 2.1-D sketch makes certain contributions to computer vision. The edge-finding stage offers a new edge-enhancing filter and a method for finding edges, ridges, and valleys using mean square gradients; these should serve as a useful addition to the standard repertoire of edge detectors. The edge-smoothing algorithm uses a fast way of finding the weighted best-fit line *or* circle to a set of edge points; this provides a new way of smoothing curves at multiple scales without shrinkage. The continuations stage offers a way of finding consistent sets of completions for disrupted contours; and the final stage finds the 2.1-D sketch for an image from a compact representation of the contour and region data. The last stage is useful primarily as an experimental tool, as it has worst-case exponential running time.

Limitations of the 2.1-D sketch algorithm.

Our algorithm has three kinds of limitations. The first comes from the fact that object outlines do not correspond well to sharp changes in image luminance. That makes it difficult to find visible object outlines from a luminance map. Although we humans think little of the task of tracing object outlines in a photograph, it clearly depends on more computation than a measure of gradient at a single scale.

The nonlinear filter cannot distinguish between shadow boundaries and real surface boundaries. It eliminates texture instead of recognizing it and it operates only at one scale. It seems that building a better filter would mean solving the problems of shadows, textures, and adaptive choice of scale. This is a recurring theme in vision–it seems one has to solve everything at once, rather than use a straightforward module by module approach.

The edge-finding algorithm is restricted for the same reasons. It uses a local measure of square directional derivative in the minimal and maximal directions, along with a hysteresis stage to extend strong edges along weak stretches. As with all edge-finding algorithms, it can be made to work well for a specific type of image (e.g., still life scenes) but we would like to see it apply to *most* images. This will require automatic choices of parameters for the scale, minimum contour length, and size of gaps to jump.

The second kind of limitation comes from the fact that continuations are computed solely from the endpoints and tangents of disrupted contours, and not from the shapes of the contours. One simple improvement would be to use the lengths of the contours as a first approximation to the scale. More sophisticated use of a set of canonical shapes would allow us to build continuations truer to the ones we seem to see. This depends on psychophysical experiments that reveal the space of expected shapes.

Finally, the third kind of limitation comes from the 2.1-D sketch *model*, which imposes a strict partial ordering on the regions in a segmentation, and which assigns a single brightness value to each region. As we have seen, self-overlapping regions and interwoven surfaces cannot be represented. If we think of the 2.1-D sketch algorithm as applying only locally, for example, to the fovial portion of a scene, then a global ordering may actually correspond to our perceptual organization. When we view an impossible figure "all at once," we tend not to perceive depth, whereas we perceive depth when viewing any consistent part of it. Thus the 2.1-D sketch may be applied to simple portions of a scene, and the results woven together at a later stage.

It is easy to remedy the limitations imposed by assigning a single brightness value to each region: replace the first term in $E_{2.1}$ by

$$\mu_1^2 \int_{R_i'} (g - \hat{g}_i)^2 d\mathbf{x} + \mu_2 \int_{R_i} \|\nabla \hat{g}_i\|^2 d\mathbf{x},$$

where $\hat{g}_i$ is a smooth function that approximates the observed brightness function g on R_i. Instead of asking that the observed intensity g have a minimum of variance on the visible part of R_i, we ask that g be approximated by a smooth function $\hat{g}_i$ on the visible part or R_i which is smooth on all of R_i, where μ_1 determines how good an approximation, and μ_2 determines how smooth.

The model is not equipped to represent three-dimensional surface shape perceived from shading, surface contours, texture density gradients, and other depth cues. We have argued that the relative depth organization of surfaces is more primal than the possible undulations and curvatures of surfaces. The former is both easier to compute and more immediately useful for segmenting a scene into areas, and eventually objects, of interest. One can think of the 2.1-D sketch as an early depth representation, with richer surface information coming at later stages.

Top-down processing

The 2.1-D sketch makes sense only under the assumption that in visual perception, we can tell what's in front of what before we figure out what's what in a scene. The continuations used for the 2.1-D sketch are based purely on the tangents and curvatures near the endpoints of visible contours and ignore the overall shapes of contours. We have seen that in human perception unfamiliar shapes still give rise to continuations and that continuations can occur that contradict the higher-level cognitive understanding of a scene.

Our theory must not assume a completely bottom-up approach that goes from raw image to contour map to segmentation. It must be combined with a certain top-down process that depends on internalized probabilities for familiar shapes. There is growing support in the community for a new theory of object recognition using bottom-up data to make top-down guesses which are then verified on the low level, in an iterative feedback loop [6, 43, 27]. The organization of unfamiliar objects may be treated less decisively at the cognitive level, but if there is higher-level input in the case of familiar objects, we can hardly expect the neocortex to shut down when it cannot find a suitable model for what it sees. Iterative feedback applies as well to finding surface organizations in an unfamiliar scene as to recognizing a familiar Dalmation in the snow.

The 2.1-D sketch could be extended to feed forward a current best-guess to higher level cognitive processes, and then use information fed back from these processes to modify, verify, or disqualify hypotheses of surface organizations.

Improvements

The ideas in this book are a first attempt at writing computer algorithms to find the organization of overlapping surfaces in a scene. As with any first attempt, the ideas are likely to be supplanted as the theory develops and better algorithms are discovered.

The curve detection stage should be coupled more tightly with the detection of endpoints and corners via the *cornerness* array. For example, the edge direction and strength fields can have associated reliability measures derived from the cornerness, so that near an endpoint, edge position, strength, and direction are considered less reliable. The same reliability measure should also be incorporated into the weights used in the best-fit algorithm for curve-smoothing, so that unreliable edge points are counted less heavily.

The curve-smoothing algorithm is an efficient method to smooth sampled contours at a fixed scale, and at the same time estimate tangent and curvature at each sample point. It does not aim to solve the general problem of reconstructing from grid-sampled versions of curves the most likely original curves under certain smoothness assumptions. One problem with the best-fit algorithm is that it minimizes an error term that penalizes distance squared from each point to the candidate circle or line. In fact, there should be no penalty at all for diverging by up to a one-half pixel distance, since each original curve point has been assigned the nearest grid point during quantization.

Nor does our curve-smoothing method reduce the storage required for the curve. David Lowe [22] has done interesting work in this direction. His method is to smooth on several scales, and replace sections of a curve with small curvature variation by circular arcs, going from larger to smaller scales. This heuristic may be applied using our fitting algorithm as well.

The continuations stage would be improved if we could find a way to interpret T-junctions consistently and accurately directly from the image brightness map. At a correctly interpreted T-junction there is only one choice of contour endpoint to continue.

The final energy-minimization stage is essentially an exponential time algorithm. It could be replaced by a much simpler algorithm that might assign ordering relations based on the T-junctions, and then group unordered pairs of regions together if their mean intensities match closely.

Finally, we would like to extend the 2.1-D sketch model to represent transparent, translucent, and similar surfaces that *modify* light as it passes through them. Shadows, for example, darken the surface on which they are cast, changing only the value of the light, but not the hue or saturation, while smoked lucite changes both the saturation and value.

Appendix A

Derivations for the Nonlinear Filter

The following derivation is given in greater detail in [35]. Consider a family of mappings

$$\Phi_\varepsilon : I_{\text{in}} \mapsto I_{\text{out}}, \quad \varepsilon > 0$$

on a fixed topological space (space of functions in our case), and suppose the limit

$$F(I) = \lim_{\varepsilon \to 0+} \frac{1}{\varepsilon} (\Phi_\varepsilon(I) - I) \tag{A.1}$$

exists and satisfies certain conditions, then the semigroup $\{\Phi_\varepsilon^N \mid N = 0, 1, 2, \ldots\}$ generated by Φ_ε approaches the 1-parameter semigroup $\{\overline{\Phi}_t \mid 0 \le t < \infty\}$ governed by the evolution equation

$$\frac{\partial \overline{\Phi}_t(I)}{\partial t} = F(\overline{\Phi}_t(I))$$

as $\varepsilon \to 0$, such that $\Phi_\varepsilon^N \to \overline{\Phi}_t$ if $\varepsilon N \to t$.

Let us consider the case where Φ_ε is defined by taking our filter, i.e., (2.1) with Q defined by (2.2), and α by (2.3); and then replacing σ^2 with $\varepsilon \sigma^2$ and α by $\varepsilon \alpha_\varepsilon$, where α_ε is a family of vector-valued functions parametrized by $\varepsilon > 0$, such that $\alpha_0 = \lim_{\varepsilon \to 0} \alpha_\varepsilon$ exists; for us it suffices to consider $\alpha_\varepsilon = (1/\sqrt{\varepsilon})\phi(\sqrt{\varepsilon}\,\mathbf{V})$ and $\alpha_0 = (c_1/\mu)\mathbf{V}$, with $\mathbf{V}$ defined as in (2.3). This parametrization is motivated by the usual heat equation with first order terms. The limit (A.1) exists, actually in a little more general configuration:

Proposition A.1 *Let $Q_{\mathbf{x}}(\cdot\,; I)$ be a positive definite quadratic form depending on $\mathbf{x} \in D$ and the intensity function I on the domain D. Let $\alpha_\varepsilon = \alpha_\varepsilon(\mathbf{x}, I)$ be a vector-valued function of $\mathbf{x}$ and I depending on $\varepsilon > 0$ such that $\alpha_0 = \lim_{\varepsilon \to 0} \alpha_\varepsilon$ exists. Define the family Φ_ε, $\varepsilon > 0$, of mappings on the space of intensity functions by*

$$\Phi_\varepsilon(I)(\mathbf{x}) = \frac{1}{Z(\mathbf{x}, \varepsilon)} \int_{D'} e^{-Q_{\mathbf{x}}(\mathbf{y}; I)/(\varepsilon \sigma^2)} I(\mathbf{x} + \mathbf{y} - \varepsilon \alpha_\varepsilon(\mathbf{x}, I)) d\mathbf{y},$$

where $D' = D - \mathbf{x} + \varepsilon \alpha_\varepsilon(\mathbf{x}, I)$ and $Z(\mathbf{x}, \varepsilon) = \int_{D'} e^{-Q_{\mathbf{x}}(\mathbf{y}; I)/(\varepsilon \sigma^2)} d\mathbf{y}$. Then we have, formally,

$$\lim_{\varepsilon \to 0+} \frac{1}{\varepsilon} (\Phi_\varepsilon(I)(\mathbf{x}) - I(\mathbf{x})) = \frac{\sigma^2}{4} \sum (Q_{\mathbf{x}, I}^{-1})_{ij} \nabla_i \nabla_j I - \alpha_0(\mathbf{x}, I) \cdot \nabla I, \tag{A.2}$$

so that $I(\,\cdot\,,t) := \lim_{\varepsilon N \to t} \Phi_\varepsilon^N(I)$ is governed by the evolution equation

$$\frac{\partial I}{\partial t}(\mathbf{x},t) = \frac{\sigma^2}{4}\sum \left(Q_{\mathbf{x},I}^{-1}\right)_{ij}\nabla_i\nabla_j I(\mathbf{x},t) - \alpha_0(\mathbf{x},I(\mathbf{x},t))\cdot\nabla_\mathbf{x} I(\mathbf{x},t), \qquad (\text{A.3})$$

where $Q_{\mathbf{x},I}$ is the symmetric matrix corresponding to $Q_\mathbf{x}(\,\cdot\,;I)$, i.e., $Q_\mathbf{x}(\mathbf{y};I) = \mathbf{y}^t Q_{\mathbf{x},I}\mathbf{y}$.

Proof: Let $d = \dim D$, so usually $d = 2$. Since $(1/\sqrt{\varepsilon})D' \to \mathbf{R}^\mathbf{d}$ as $\varepsilon \to 0$, and since

$$\exp(-Q_\mathbf{x}(\mathbf{y};I)/(\varepsilon\sigma^2)) = \exp(-Q_\mathbf{x}(\mathbf{y}/\sqrt{\varepsilon};I)/\sigma^2),$$

by letting $\mathbf{Y} := \mathbf{y}/\sqrt{\varepsilon}$ we have

$$\int_{D'} e^{-Q_\mathbf{x}(\mathbf{y};I)/(\varepsilon\sigma^2)}I(\mathbf{x}+\mathbf{y}-\varepsilon\alpha_\varepsilon(\mathbf{x},I))d\mathbf{y}$$

$$= \varepsilon^{d/2}\int_{(1/\sqrt{\varepsilon})D'} e^{-Q_\mathbf{x}(\mathbf{Y};I)/(\sigma^2)}I(\mathbf{x}+\sqrt{\varepsilon}\mathbf{Y}-\varepsilon\alpha_\varepsilon(\mathbf{x},I))d\mathbf{Y}$$

$$\cong \varepsilon^{d/2}\int_{\mathbf{R}^\mathbf{d}} e^{-Q_\mathbf{x}(\mathbf{Y};I)/(\sigma^2)}\left(1+\frac{\varepsilon}{2}\sum_{i,j}Y_iY_j\nabla_i\nabla_j\right)I(\mathbf{x}-\varepsilon\alpha_\varepsilon(\mathbf{x},I))d\mathbf{Y}$$

and

$$Z(\mathbf{x},\varepsilon) \cong \varepsilon^{d/2}\int_{\mathbf{R}^\mathbf{d}} e^{-Q_\mathbf{x}(\mathbf{Y};I)/\sigma^2}d\mathbf{Y}$$

as $\varepsilon \to 0$. So we have

$$\frac{\Phi_\varepsilon(I)(\mathbf{x}) - I(\mathbf{x})}{\varepsilon}$$

$$= \frac{\Phi_\varepsilon(I)(\mathbf{x}) - I(\mathbf{x}-\varepsilon\alpha_\varepsilon(\mathbf{x},I))}{\varepsilon} + \frac{I(\mathbf{x}-\varepsilon\alpha_\varepsilon(\mathbf{x},I)) - I(\mathbf{x})}{\varepsilon}$$

$$\cong \frac{\int_{\mathbf{R}^\mathbf{d}} e^{-Q_\mathbf{x}(\mathbf{Y};I)/\sigma^2}\frac{1}{2}\sum_{i,j}Y_iY_j\nabla_i\nabla_j I(\mathbf{x}-\varepsilon\alpha_\varepsilon(\mathbf{x},I))d\mathbf{Y}}{\int_{\mathbf{R}^\mathbf{d}} e^{-Q_\mathbf{x}(\mathbf{Y};I)/\sigma^2}d\mathbf{Y}} - \alpha_\varepsilon(\mathbf{x},I)\cdot\nabla I$$

$$\cong \frac{\int_{\mathbf{R}^\mathbf{d}} e^{-Q_\mathbf{x}(\mathbf{Y};I)/\sigma^2}\frac{1}{2}\sum_{i,j}Y_iY_j\nabla_i\nabla_j I(\mathbf{x})d\mathbf{Y}}{\int_{\mathbf{R}^\mathbf{d}} e^{-Q_\mathbf{x}(\mathbf{Y};I)/\sigma^2}d\mathbf{Y}} - \alpha_\varepsilon(\mathbf{x},I)\cdot\nabla I$$

$$\cong \frac{1}{2}\sum_{i,j}c_{ij}(Q_\mathbf{x}(\,\cdot\,;I))\nabla_i\nabla_j I(\mathbf{x}) - \alpha_\varepsilon(\mathbf{x},I)\cdot\nabla I$$

$$\cong \frac{1}{2}\sum_{i,j}c_{ij}(Q_\mathbf{x}(\,\cdot\,;I))\nabla_i\nabla_j I(\mathbf{x}) - \alpha_0(\mathbf{x},I)\cdot\nabla I$$

as $\varepsilon \to 0$, where

$$c_{ij}(Q) := \int_{\mathbf{R}^\mathbf{d}} e^{-Q(\mathbf{Y})}Y_iY_j d\mathbf{Y} \Big/ \int_{\mathbf{R}^\mathbf{d}} e^{-Q(\mathbf{Y})}d\mathbf{Y}$$

for a positive definite quadratic form Q. Using the diagonalization of Q and

$$\int_{-\infty}^{\infty} e^{-x^2} x^2 dx = \frac{1}{2} \int_{-\infty}^{\infty} e^{-x^2} dx$$

(integration by parts), we obtain $c_{ij}(Q) = (Q^{-1})_{ij}/2$, and hence (A.2).　　　■

Remark 1.2 The proposition is stated without specifying the space of functions to which I belongs. This is not a problem in the discrete model. In the continuous model the condition for I should be specified to make the calculations valid. For example, I can be any function such that $Q_{\mathbf{x}}(\mathbf{y}; I)$ and $\alpha_\epsilon(\mathbf{x}, I)$ are well-defined and are C^∞ in $\mathbf{x}$. If $Q_{\mathbf{x}}(\mathbf{y}; I)$ is defined by (2.2) and

$$Q'_{\mathbf{x}_0}(\mathbf{y}) = \int \rho_2(\xi - \mathbf{x}_0) q(\mathbf{y}; \xi) d\xi$$

$$= \int \rho_2(\xi - \mathbf{x}_0)(\nabla I_{\text{in}}(\xi) \cdot \mathbf{y})^2 d\xi \tag{A.4}$$

where ρ_1 and ρ_2 are cut-off functions, so that $\int k(\mathbf{x}_0, \mathbf{x}) d\mathbf{x} = 1$; and if $\alpha_\epsilon(\mathbf{x}, I) = (1/\sqrt{\epsilon})\phi(\sqrt{\epsilon} V)$, $\mathbf{V}$ is defined by (2.3) and

$$\phi(V) = c_1 V / \sqrt{\mu^2 + V^2}, \tag{A.5}$$

this means only that $\nabla I \in L^2_{\text{loc}}(D)$ (i.e., $\|\nabla I\|^2$ is locally integrable) and (if D is unbounded) of moderate growth. The condition that $\nabla I \in L^2_{\text{loc}}(D)$ can be relaxed to allow infinitely sharp edges. The equation (A.3) becomes a nonlinear integro-differential equation with the finite (nonzero) window size as a characteristic length scale.

　　The combination of the zero kernel size with a finite window size is motivated by physical insight into the algorithm as a simulated heat flow: the kernel size should be zero since the heat flow should be affected by the heat conduction coefficients only pointwise. The finite window size allows heat conduction coefficients to depend on the heat distribution nearby, and hence vary smoothly. Thus (A.3) may be considered as a regularization of the differential equation (A.8) obtained from (A.3) as the window size $\to 0$.

Limit as spatial scale $\to 0$

To consider the limit as the spatial scale $\to 0$, we let the support of the cut-off functions ρ_2 and ρ_3 shrink to a point, e.g., replace $\rho_i(\mathbf{y})$ by $\delta^{-d}\rho_i(\delta^{-1}\mathbf{y})$ (d is the dimension of the space), and then let $\delta \to 0$. The integral signs in (A.4) and (2.3) disappear, so (2.2) becomes

$$Q_{\mathbf{x}_0}(\mathbf{y}) = A\|\mathbf{y}\|^2 + (\nabla I_{\text{in}}(\mathbf{x}_0) \cdot \mathbf{y})^2,$$

and the corresponding symmetric matrix will become

$$Q_{\mathbf{x}_0, I} = A\mathbf{Id} + \nabla I_{\text{in}}(\mathbf{x}_0) \otimes \nabla I_{\text{in}}(\mathbf{x}_0),$$

where $\mathbf{Id}$ is the identity matrix, and for any (column) vector $\mathbf{v} = (v_i)$, $\mathbf{v} \otimes \mathbf{v}$ is the square matrix $\mathbf{v}\mathbf{v}^t = (v_i v_j)$. We have the following

Lemma A.3

$$Q_{x,I}^{-1} = \frac{1}{A}\left(\mathbf{Id} - \frac{1}{A + \|\nabla I\|^2}\nabla I \otimes \nabla I\right),\qquad(A.6)$$

$$\sum (Q_{x,I}^{-1})_{ij}\nabla_i\nabla_j I = \frac{1}{A}\left(\Delta I - \frac{\sum_{i,j}\nabla_i I\nabla_j I\nabla_i\nabla_j I}{A + \|\nabla I\|^2}\right).\qquad(A.7)$$

Proof: Since (A.7) follows from (A.6), and since both side of (A.6) are rational in A, it suffices to prove (A.6) assuming $A \gg 0$. By Neumann series expansion, we have

$$
\begin{aligned}
Q_{x,I}^{-1} &= (A\mathbf{Id} + \nabla I \otimes \nabla I)^{-1} \\
&= \frac{1}{A}\sum_{i=0}^{\infty}(-1)^i\frac{1}{A^i}(\nabla I \otimes \nabla I)^i \\
&= \frac{1}{A}\left[\mathbf{Id} + \sum_{i=0}^{\infty}(-1)^i\frac{\|\nabla I\|^{2i-1}}{A^i}(\nabla I \otimes \nabla I)\right]
\end{aligned}
$$

using $(\mathbf{v} \otimes \mathbf{v})^i = \|\mathbf{v}\|^{2(i-1)}\mathbf{v} \otimes \mathbf{v}$ for $i > 0$. Summing up the geometric series, we obtain (A.6). ∎

To see the limit of the displacement term α_0 as ρ_3 is scaled to concentrate around the origin, for simplicity we consider the special case where

$$\frac{1}{|\mathbf{y}|}\rho_3^\delta(\mathbf{y}) = \pi^{-d/2}\delta^{-d-2}e^{-\|y\|^2/\delta^2}.$$

Then by integration by parts, we have

$$
\begin{aligned}
\alpha_0 &= \frac{c_1}{\mu}\int(\mathbf{y}\cdot\nabla I)\nabla I\frac{1}{|\mathbf{y}|}\rho_3^\delta(\mathbf{y})d\mathbf{y} \\
&= \frac{\delta^2 c_1}{2\mu}\int\sum_i\nabla_i(\nabla_i I\nabla I)\frac{1}{|\mathbf{y}|}\rho_3^\delta(\mathbf{y})d\mathbf{y} \\
&\cong \frac{c_1}{2\mu}\sum_i\nabla_i(\nabla_i I\nabla I)
\end{aligned}
$$

as $\delta \to 0$. So we have

$$\alpha_0(\mathbf{x}, I) \to \frac{c_1}{2\mu}\left(\Delta I\cdot\nabla I + \sum(\nabla_i I\cdot\nabla_i)\nabla I\right)\qquad\text{as}\qquad\delta\to 0.$$

Combining all these, we obtain

Proposition A.4 *As $\delta \to 0$, the equation $(A.3)$ approaches*

$$\frac{\partial I}{\partial t} = \frac{\sigma^2}{4}\frac{1}{A}\left(\Delta I - \frac{\sum\nabla_i I\nabla_j I\nabla_i\nabla_j I}{A + \|\nabla I\|^2}\right) - \frac{c_1}{2\mu}\left(\Delta I\cdot\|\nabla I\|^2 + \sum_{i,j}\nabla_i I\cdot\nabla_j I\cdot\nabla_i\nabla_j I\right). \quad(A.8)$$

Appendix B

Program Code

This section describes the filter algorithm and the contour tracing algorithm in enough detail for a programmer to code them. They are given in pseudo-C code that resembles the C language. The later programs that reconstruct the 2.1-D sketch are not included because they are intended only to demonstrate that the concepts are valid using brute-force combinatoric search. Readers with access to the internet may obtain the actual C code used for the experiments in this book via anonymous ftp from the internet host `math.harvard.edu` in the directory `vision`.

For simplicity, the pseudo-code treats all images as two-dimensional arrays $I(x, y)$, $x \in \{0, \ldots, \text{width} - 1\}$, $y \in \{0, \ldots, \text{height} - 1\}$, with real-valued samples. All so-called `real` variables are stored in IEEE standard single-precision floating point format.

The pseudo-code does not deal with the borders of images explicitly. Where appropriate, we simulate reflecting the image at the borders, so $I(-1, \cdot) = I(1, \cdot)$, and so on, analogously on the right side and top and bottom. This makes it possible to calculate derivatives and apply kernels to pixels near the border. We do this with index arrays $R(-k \ldots \text{height} + k)$ for the rows, and $C(-k \ldots \text{width} + k)$ for the columns, and then access the image using $I(C(x), R(y))$. This adds two array references to each pixel access. Others may find it more effective to ignore pixels near the borders, or to copy I into a larger array and fill the borders with the reflected values.

B.1 Nonlinear filter

In the following implementation of the nonlinear filter, we use a number of time-saving short-cuts. We fix ρ_2 and ρ_3 to be identical Gaussian bumps of standard deviation τ; there is no parameter M. The other parameters are N (we build an $N \times N$ sampled kernel at each point), σ^2 and μ as described above.

1. Compute E, F, and G.

We create three new arrays, $E(x, y)$, $F(x, y)$, and $G(x, y)$, containing I_x^2, $I_x I_y$ and I_y^2 respectively, estimated by taking the symmetric difference of nearest neighbors:

$$I_x(x, y) \simeq (I(x + 1, y) - I(x - 1, y))/2, \text{ and}$$
$$I_y(x, y) \simeq (I(x, y + 1) - I(x, y - 1))/2.$$

We then blur the arrays E, F and G by a discrete convolution with the kernel defined by $k(x)k(y)$ where

$$k(r) = \frac{1}{\text{norm}} \cdot \begin{cases} e^{-r^2/2\tau^2} & \text{for } |r| \leq 2\tau, \\ \frac{1}{16e^2}(4 - \frac{|r|}{\tau})^4 & \text{for } 2\tau < |r| \leq 4\tau, \text{ and} \\ 0 & \text{otherwise} \end{cases}$$

where norm is a normalizing factor that makes the discrete kernel sum to 1. This is a twice continuously differentiable Gaussian bump with its tails gracefully splined to zero. Simply truncating the tails of a Gaussian introduces terrifically important–and elusive–errors in the second derivatives.

The blurring is performed "separably": first the rows are blurred, then the columns, using a kernel with $\lceil 4\tau \rceil + 1$ samples, with $k(0)$ at the center.

2. Compute the kernel for (x, y).

The displacement term α at $x_0 = (x, y)$ can be approximated to first order very easily and quickly from E and G. Recall that α was given by

$$\alpha(x_0) = \phi(\mathbf{V}),$$

$$\mathbf{V} = \int_U \frac{1}{|\mathbf{y}|}(\nabla I(x_0 + \mathbf{y}) \cdot \mathbf{y})\nabla I(x_0 + \mathbf{y})\rho_3(\mathbf{y})d\mathbf{y}, \tag{B.1}$$

where ρ_3 is a cut-off function supported on U, c is a constant, and ϕ compresses $\mathbf{V}$ to limit displacement: $\phi(\mathbf{V}) = c_1\mathbf{V}/\sqrt{\mu^2 + \mathbf{V}^2}$, with $c_1 \approx (1/4)$·kernel size.

Recall that we fixed ρ_3 to be a guassian with standard deviation τ: $e^{-(x^2+y^2)/2\tau^2}$.

Using a first order approximation, it is enough to compute

$$\mathbf{V} \sim \frac{1}{2}(\frac{\partial}{\partial x}E + \frac{\partial}{\partial y}F, \frac{\partial}{\partial x}F + \frac{\partial}{\partial y}G).$$

The partials can be approximated by the symmetric difference of nearest neighbors, as for I_x, etc., above. In this way it is just as fast to compute $\mathbf{V}$ at each point as building a new image to hold the value of $\mathbf{V}$ everywhere at once, so no further arrays are necessary.

We finish computing the displacement term $-\alpha = (P, Q)$, and combine it with the triple (E, F, G) at (x, y) to sample the displaced kernel in an $N \times N$ area with $(0, 0)$ at the center.

$$K(x, y) = \frac{1}{\text{norm}}e^{-(Ex^2+2Fxy+Gy^2+Px+Qy)}$$

with norm $= \sum_{(z,w)\in N \times N} e^{-(Ez^2+2Fzw+Gw^2+Pz+Qw)}$. Note also that the kernel need not be precomputed into an array as long as the norm is computed incrementally when the kernel is applied.

3. Apply the kernel

The result is $I_{\text{out}}(x, y) = \sum_{(z,w)\in N \times N} K(z, w)I(x, y)$.

Filter code

filter

The main filter function: returns a new image containing the filtered input.

```
IMAGE
filter(I, N, sigma, tau, mu)
IMAGE I;          /* input image */
int N;            /* width for the blurring kernels */
real sigma;       /* overall broadness of the blurring kernels */
real tau;         /* gradient window size */
real mu;          /* displacement attenuation */
{
    IMAGE Iout;
    real x, y, dx, dy, ex, fx, fy, gy, p, q;
    IMAGE E, F, G;

    /* Compute approximate I_x^2, I_x I_y, and I_y^2. */
    FOR_EACH_PIXEL(x,y) {
        dx = (I[x+1][y] - I[x-1][y]) / 2;
        dy = (I[x][y+1] - I[x][y-1]) / 2;
        E[x][y] = dx*dx;
        F[x][y] = dx*dy;
        G[x][y] = dy*dy;
    }

    /* Blur with splined Gaussian. */
    blur(E, tau);
    blur(F, tau);
    blur(G, tau);

#    define    phi(x) (N/4)*x / sqrt(mu*mu + x*x)

    FOR_EACH_PIXEL(x,y) {
        ex = (E[x+1][y] - E[x-1][y]) / 2;
        fx = (F[x+1][y] - F[x-1][y]) / 2;
        fy = (F[x][y+1] - F[x][y-1]) / 2;
        gy = (G[x][y+1] - G[x][y-1]) / 2;
        p = phi((ex + fy)/2);
        q = phi((fx + gy)/2);
        Iout[x][y] = filter_point(I,x,y,
                                  E[x][y], F[x][y], G[x][y],
                                  p, q, N, sigma, mu);
    }

    return Iout;
}
```

filter_point

Returns the new value after filtering centered at (x, y).

```
real
filter_point(I, x, y, e, f, g, p, q, N, sigma, mu)
IMAGE I;
real x,y;           /* current pixel location of filtering */
real e,f,g,p,q;     /* shape and displacement of kernel */
int N;              /* width of blurring kernel */
real sigma;         /* breadth of the kernel */
real mu;            /* displacement attenuation */
{
    real dx, dy, r, v, norm, total;

    r = (int) (N-1)/2;
    norm = total = 0;

    for (dx = -r; dx <= r; dx++)
    for (dy = -r; dy <= r; dy++) {
        v = exp(-(e*dx*dx
                + 2*f*dx*dy
                + g*dy*dy + px+qy)/2*sigma*sigma);
        total = total + v * I[x+dx][y+dy];
        norm = norm + v;
    }

    return total / norm;
}
```

blur

Blurs an image separably with a Gaussian bump with tails gracefully splined to zero. Replaces the contents of I. KER is $\lceil 4\sigma \rceil$.

```
void
blur(I, sigma)
IMAGE I;
real sigma;        /* standard-deviation, as in e^{-(x²+y²)/2σ²} */
{
    IMAGE J;           /* intermediate copy of I */
    real k[-KER...KER]; /* kernel */
    int x;
    real norm;
```

```
/* Build the kernel in k */
norm = 0;
for (x = -KER; x <= KER; x++) {
    if (abs(x) <= 2*sigma)
        k[x] = exp(-x*x/2*sigma*sigma);
    else if (2*sigma < abs(x) && abs(x) <= 4*sigma)
        k[x] = 1/(16*M_E*M_E) * pow(4-abs(x)/sigma, 4);
    else
        k[x] = 0;
    norm = norm + k[x];
}

for (x = -KER; x <= KER; x++)
    k[x] = k[x]/norm;

/* Apply the kernel separately in each dimension */
convolve1d(I,J,k,KER,Vertical);
convolve1d(J,I,k,KER,Horizontal);
}
```

convolve1d

Convolves image I with kernel k along axis putting result in J.

```
void
convolve1d(I,J,k,a,axis)
IMAGE I, J;      /* input and output images */
real k[];        /* 1-dim kernel */
int a;           /* k[-a ... a] */
{
    int x,y,i,dx,dy;
    real total;

    if (axis == Horizontal) {
        FOR_EACH_PIXEL(x,y) {
            total = 0;
            for (i = -a; i <= a; i++)
                total = total + k[i] * I[x][y+i];

            J[x][y] = total;
        }
    } else {
        /* Vertical */
        FOR_EACH_PIXEL(x,y) {
            total = 0;
            for (i = -a; i <= a; i++)
                total = total + k[i] * I[x][y+i];
```

```
          J[x][y] = total;
      }
   }
}
```

B.2   Edge tracing

This code detects edges and corners, completing disrupted edges across small gaps. It yields a linked list of Contour structures, each of which gives a list of points that can be traced in the pixel map PMap. These contours meet only at their endpoints.

Data Structures

```
typedef struct { real x,y; } vector;
typedef struct { int x,y; } PixelPos;

typedef struct Contour {          /* an "edge" */
    struct Contour *R;            /* next in linked list */
    int        length;            /* number of pixels */
    boolean    closed;            /* closed curve */
    boolean    split;             /* closed and HEAD is corner point */
    boolean    boundary;          /* part of image boundary */
    PixelPos end[2];              /* the two ends */
#              define  HEAD  0
#              define  TAIL  1
} Contour;

typedef struct ContourPoint {     /* one point of one contour */
    Contour *con;
    real       angle;             /* (radians) edge tangent angle */
    Neighbor n[2];                /* directions to next/prev pixels in PMap */
#              define FWD  0       /* n[0] takes you forward */
#              define BACK 1
} ContourPoint;

typedef struct PixelInfo {        /* one pixel in the PMap */
    enum {
        P_EMPTY, P_POINT, P_END, P_MIDDLE,
        P_CORNER, P_T, P_Y, P_X,
    } type;
    vector  pos;                  /* real-valued coordinate position */
    real       k;                 /* curvature if this is a P_MIDDLE point */
    ContourPoint conpt[4];
} PixelInfo;
```

Global Variables

```
Contour *Contours;             /* linked list of contours */
IMAGE   Strength;              /* edge strength at each pixel */
IMAGE   Edgex, Edgey;          /* edge direction */
IMAGE   Cornerness;            /* see Operators() */
PixelInfo *PMap[Height][Width]; /* the pixel map of con's at each pix */
```

TraceContours

This is the main function which builds the global Contours list.

```
TraceContours(I, SDev, SweepAngle,
              MaxJumpGap, TooShort, MinUntethered,
              LoPct, HiPct, CornerRadius, CornerPct,
              OutlineBorder, PruneCrackTips)
IMAGE    I;              /* input */
real     SDev;           /* std dev in pixel widths – sets length scales */
real     SweepAngle;     /* gap-jumping spread at endpoints */
real     MaxJumpGap;     /* distance of largest gap to jump in pixel widths */
real     TooShort;       /* kill contours < TooShort before gap-jumping */
real     MinUntethered;  /* elim. untethered contours < this many pixels */
real     LoPct, HiPct;   /* edge detection thresholds in percentile */
real     CornerRadius;   /* radius for local max corner measure */
real     CornerPct;      /* threshold for cornerness in percentile */
boolean OutlineBorder;   /* the image border is considered a contour */
boolean PruneCrackTips;  /* all must meet significant contours at both ends */
{
     real CornerThresh, Lo, Hi;

     Operators(I);  /* edge strength & direction, corner strength */

     /* set thresholds */
     Lo = ThreshPct(Strength, Height * Width, LoPct);
     Hi = ThreshPct(Strength, Height * Width, HiPct);
     CornerThresh = ThreshPct(Cornerness,
                              Height * Width, CornerPct);

     /* Trace edges, linking up ContourPoints */
     if (OutlineBorder)
          DrawBorder(0);
     BuildPixelMap(SDev, Lo, Hi);

     DeleteShort(TooShort);
     MergeCorners();

     /* split contours at corners */
     FindCorners(CornerThresh, CornerRadius);
```

```
/* reflect at ends to join up with neighbors. */
GrowContours(MaxJumpGap);

if (MinUntethered > 1)
    DeleteUntethered(MinUntethered);

/* and delete stray contours that end off in nowhere */
if (PruneCrackTips)
    DeleteStray(MinUntethered);

/* corner detection */
MergeCorners();
FindCorners(CornerThresh, CornerRadius);

/* return or print Contours, tracing each from HEAD to TAIL */
}
```

Operators

Compute edge strength, cornerness, and edge direction using the Nitzberg/Shiota filtering technique of summing I_x^2, I_y^2, and $I_x I_y$ in a window (here we just blur with Gaussian). Shorter eigenvalue gives cornerness; corresponding eigenvector gives edge direction; and sqrt(sum of eigenvalues) gives edge strength.

```
Operators(I)
IMAGE  I;
{
    int     y, x;
    real  disc, a, b, c, e1, e2;
    real  vx, vy, length;
    IMAGE  Gradx = NULL, Grady = NULL;
    IMAGE  Ix2, IxIy, Iy2;

    /* Compute approximate Ix², IxIy, and Iy². */
    FOR_EACH_PIXEL(x,y) {
        dx = (I[x+1][y] - I[x-1][y]) / 2;
        dy = (I[x][y+1] - I[x][y-1]) / 2;
        Ix2[x][y] = dx*dx;
        IxIy[x][y] = dx*dy;
        Iy2[x][y] = dy*dy;
    }

    /* Blur with splined Gaussian--see filter pseudo-code. */
    blur(Ix2, SDev);
    blur(IxIy, SDev);
    blur(Iy2, SDev);
```

```
/* get eigenvalues; fill edge and corner arrays */
FOR_EACH_PIXEL(x,y) {
        a = Ix2[x][y];
        b = IxIy[x][y];
        c = Iy2[x][y];

        /* eigenvalues */
        disc = sqrt(a*a + 4*b*b - 2*a*c + c*c);
        e1 = (a + c - disc) / 2;
        e2 = (a + c + disc) / 2;

        /* |shorter eigenvalue| indicates cornerness */
        Cornerness[x][y] = fabs(e1);

        /* sqrt(e1/e2) gives eccentricity (ignore) */
        Strength[x][y] = sqrt(a + c);

        /* tangent to edge = +/- eigenvector corresp to e1 normalized */
        vx = -b;
        vy = a - e1;
        length = sqrt(vx*vx + vy*vy);
        if (length != 0) {
                vx /= length;
                vy /= length;
        } else
                vx = vy = 0;
        Edgex[x][y] = vx;
        Edgey[x][y] = vy;
    }
}
```

BuildPixelMap

This is the main function that builds contours starting from each strong edge point.

```
BuildPixelMap(SDev, Lo, Hi)
real SDev;        /* length scale */
real Lo, Hi;      /* edge strength thresholds */
{
    int        x, y;
    FirstPass = TRUE;
    FOR_EACH_PIXEL(x,y)
        if (PMap[x][y] == NULL && LocalMax(x, y, Hi))
            BuildContour(x, y, SDev, Lo);
    FirstPass = FALSE;
}
```

BuildContour

This function builds a new contour structure starting at point (x,y) and adds it to the
Contours list. Walks along neighboring edge points that are above the Lo threshold, and
whose edge tangent is near parallel to the tail. After it's all over, tries to grow in the other
direction.

```
BuildContour(x, y, SDev, Lo)
int     x, y;
real    SDev;       /* length scale */
real    Lo;         /* edge strength threshold */
{
    Contour *con;
    ContourPoint *conpt;
    PixelInfo *p;

    con = NewContour(x, y);
    TraceContour(con, Lo, 0);   /* last direction = none */

    if (!con->closed) {
        ReverseContour(con);

        /* last direction = delta from 2nd to 1st pt */
        GetEnd(con, HEAD, &conpt, &p);
        GetNext(con, HEAD, &conpt, &p);

        if (conpt == NULL)
            return;                 /* a 1-point contour */
        TraceContour(con, SDev, Lo, (int) conpt->n[BACK]);
    }

    /* kill the contour if the whole thing is next to the image boundary */
    if (OutlineBorder)
        NotNearBoundary(con, SDev);
}
```

ThreshPct

Threshold given percentile: finds the value V for which a given percent of pixels have
values < V.

```
#define HISTOGRAM           1000        /* no. of intervals for real-line histogram */
real
ThreshPct(array, nelt, percentile)
real    *array;
int     nelt;
real    percentile;
{
```

```
int         histogram[HISTOGRAM];
int         i, interval;
real        thresh;
int         marker, sum;
real        min, max;

/* get min and max values */
min = max = array[0];
for (i = 1; i < nelt; i++) {
    if (min > array[i])
        min = array[i];
    if (max < array[i])
        max = array[i];
}

/* divide [min,max] into HISTOGRAM equal intervals */
for (i = 0; i < HISTOGRAM; i++)
    histogram[i] = 0;
for (i = 1; i < nelt; i++) {
    interval = (int) 0.5 +
        (array[i] - min) * HISTOGRAM / (max - min);
    if (interval == HISTOGRAM)
        interval--;
    histogram[interval]++;
}

/* mark percentile by number of pixels not to be exceeded */
marker = nelt * percentile / 100.0;
for (i = 0, sum = 0; i < HISTOGRAM && sum < marker; i++)
    sum += histogram[i];
thresh = min + (i - 1) * (max - min) / HISTOGRAM;
return thresh;
}
#undef HISTOGRAM
```

LocalMax

Returns TRUE if this point is a significant contour point, that is, a be local maximum of
edge strength in the +/-grad directions, with Strength >= thresh.

```
*/
boolean
LocalMax(ax, ay, thresh)
int      ax, ay;
real     thresh;
{
    real     x, y, mag;
    real     a, b, c, d, adjusted, maxc, minc, absx, absy;
```

```
mag = Strength[ax][ay];
if (mag <= thresh)
    return FALSE;
if (ay == 0 || ay == Height - 1 || ax == 0 || ax == Width - 1)
    return FALSE;

/* Edgex, Edgey give tangent to edge; use perp. */
x = Edgey[ax][ay];
y = -Edgex[ax][ay];
absx = ABS(x);
absy = ABS(y);

/* four cases */
if (absx < absy) {
    maxc = absy;
    minc = absx;
    b = Strength[ax][ay - 1];
    c = Strength[ax][ay + 1];
} else {
    maxc = absx;
    minc = absy;
    b = Strength[ax - 1][ay];
    c = Strength[ax + 1][ay];
}

if (x * y > 0) {                 /* same sign */
    /* case 1 or 3 - */
    a = Strength[ax - 1][ay - 1];
    d = Strength[ax + 1][ay + 1];
} else {

    if (absx < absy) {
        /* case 2 - steep / */
        a = Strength[ax + 1][ay - 1];
        d = Strength[ax - 1][ay + 1];
    } else {
        /* case 4 - shallow / */
        a = Strength[ax - 1][ay + 1];
        d = Strength[ax + 1][ay - 1];
    }
}

adjusted = (maxc + minc) * mag;
if (adjusted > maxc * b + minc * a
    && adjusted > maxc * c + minc * d)
    return TRUE;
return FALSE;
}
```

NotNearBoundary

Deletes a contour if too close to the image boundary.

```
NotNearBoundary(c, SDev)
Contour *c;
real SDev;
{
    ContourPoint *conpt;
    PixelInfo *p;
    real        totaldist = 0.0;
    int         npoints = 0;

    for (GetEnd(c, HEAD, &conpt, &p); conpt != NULL;
         GetNext(c, FWD, &conpt, &p)) {
        real  dtop, dbot, dleft, dright, dmin;

        dtop = MAX((p->pos.y - 0) - 1, 0);
        dbot = MAX((Height - 1 - p->pos.y) - 1, 0);
        dleft = MAX((p->pos.x - 0) - 1, 0);
        dright = MAX((Width - 1 - p->pos.x) - 1, 0);
        dmin = dtop;

        if (dmin > dbot)
            dmin = dbot;
        if (dmin > dleft)
            dmin = dleft;
        if (dmin > dright)
            dmin = dright;
        totaldist += dmin;
        npoints++;
    }

    if (totaldist < SDev * npoints)
        DeleteContour(c);
}
```

TraceContour

Trace a contour "backwards", i.e., adding successive pixels to the HEAD of the contour. curdir is the neighbor direction in which we last moved. con must be structurally consistent.

```
#define HUGE_PENALTY    1.0e10 /* an impossibly large penalty */
```

```
TraceContour(con, SDev, Lo, curdir)
Contour *con;
real    SDev;
real    Lo;
int     curdir;
{
     int        x, y, dir, bestdir, n;
     real       compat, bestcompat;      /* compatibility: lower is better */
     PixelPos   dirvec, pix;
     PixelInfo *p, *curp;                /* for candidate and current */
     ContourPoint *curconpt;             /* "current" point */

     /* the 8 or 5 neighbors to visit given you just moved in dir curdir */
     static char neighbors[NEIGHBORS][NEIGHBORS] = {
          1, 2, 3, 4, 5, 6, 7, 8, 0,     /* 1st pixel looks all around */
          7, 8, 1, 2, 3, 0, 0, 0, 0,     /* Note: */
          8, 1, 2, 3, 4, 0, 0, 0, 0,     /* 4 3 2 */
          1, 2, 3, 4, 5, 0, 0, 0, 0,     /* 5 0 1 */
          2, 3, 4, 5, 6, 0, 0, 0, 0,     /* 6 7 8 */
          3, 4, 5, 6, 7, 0, 0, 0, 0,     /* Example: */
          4, 5, 6, 7, 8, 0, 0, 0, 0,     /* if you last moved 1 (right) */
          5, 6, 7, 8, 1, 0, 0, 0, 0,     /* next move can be 7,8,1,2,3 */
          6, 7, 8, 1, 2, 0, 0, 0, 0,
     };

     pix = con->end[HEAD];

     /* set current ptr into PMap */
     GetEnd(con, HEAD, &curconpt, &curp);

     for (;;) {
          GetEnd(con, HEAD, &curconpt, &curp);

          /* link to best nearest neighbor with near parallel tan */
          bestdir = -1;
          bestcompat = HUGE_PENALTY;

          /* cycle over plausible neighbors given we're headed curdir */
          for (n = 0; (dir = neighbors[curdir][n]) != 0; n++) {
               dirvec = NeighborPos[dir];
               x = dirvec.x + pix.x;
               y = dirvec.y + pix.y;

               /* non-maximum supression */
               if (!LocalMax(x, y, Lo))
                    continue;
```

```
                    /* Can't double back on ourselves too quickly */
                    if ((p = PMap[x][y]) != NULL
                        && CONPT(p, con) != NO_CONTOUR
                        && StepsToEnd(p, HEAD, con) < MIN_CLOSED)
                        continue;


                    /* compatibility: [0,1 or so], lower is better */
                    compat = Compatible(/* vector cur to next */
                                        pptovec(dirvec),
                                        /* tan at cur */
                                        v_vec(Edgex[pix.x][pix.y],
                                              Edgey[pix.x][pix.y]),
                                        /* tan at next */
                                        v_vec(Edgex[x][y],
                                              Edgey[x][y]));


                    if (bestdir == -1 || compat < bestcompat) {
                        bestdir = dir;
                        bestcompat = compat;
                    }
                }


                if (bestdir == -1)
                        return;                 /* nothing to do */


                dir = bestdir;


                /* set pix and (x,y) to the new candidate neighbor */
                x = pix.x += NeighborPos[dir].x;
                y = pix.y += NeighborPos[dir].y;


                /* Finish inserting - return TRUE if hit end */
                if (AddPoint(con, HEAD, (real) x, (real) y))
                        return;
                curdir = dir;                   /* remember which way we just went */
        }
}
```

AddPoint

Adds pixel (x,y) to end of contour con. Returns TRUE if this created a Y, T, Corner or closed contour rather than an End; FALSE otherwise

```
boolean
AddPoint(con, end, rx, ry)
Contour *con;
int     end;
real    rx, ry;
{
    ContourPoint *conpt, *endconpt;
    PixelInfo *p, *endp;
    int         dir;                    /* direction from (x,y) to end of con */
    int         ix = IROUND(rx);
    int         iy = IROUND(ry);
    PixelPos pos;


    /* neighbor direction from end of con to (ix,iy) */
    pos.x = ix;
    pos.y = iy;
    dir = WayToNhbr(con->end[end], pos);
    if (dir == 0)
        return TRUE;  /* not a neighbor; contour ends here */


    /* check for pixel info at new candidate point */
    if ((p = PMap[ix][iy]) != NULL && p->type != P_EMPTY) {


        /* We've just run into another contour (or self) */
        JoinContour(con, end, p);
        return TRUE;
    }


    /* new point */
    if (p == NULL)          /* don't make new if already there empty */
        p = PMap[ix][iy] = NewPixelInfo(ix, iy);


    GetEnd(con, end, &endconpt, &endp);
    /* update this point before doing next */
    if (endp->type == P_POINT)
        endp->type = P_END;
    else if (endp->type == P_END)
        endp->type = P_MIDDLE;
    else                                /* adding to a contour that ended in a Y? */
        assert(0); /* fail */
```

```
    /* point end of con towards new pixel; make new pixel new end of con */
    endconpt->n[end == HEAD ? BACK : FWD] = dir;
    p->type = P_END;
    p->pos.x = rx;
    p->pos.y = ry;
    con->end[end] = pos;          /* this becomes the new end */
    con->length++;
    conpt = &p->conpt[0];
    conpt->con = con;             /* contour pointer is con */

    /* point new pixel to old end */
    conpt->n[end == HEAD ? FWD : BACK] = AntiNhbr[dir];
    return FALSE;
}
```

Compatible

Returns a measure of compatibility given two points with tangents; a likelihood that they are part of the same contour. Given vectors v, v1, and v2 with v running from the base of v1 to the base of v2, $|v|$ is the distance between the points. The sin of the angle between v1 and v2 is sinv1v2. Penalty value is given by the following: For nearby points the penalty is

$$\text{nearby penalty} = |\text{sinv1v2}| + \text{SPL}|v|$$

SPL is a tradeoff constant that gives sin of angle per unit length. Thus a point farther away is more compatible only if the angle between its tangent and the candidate's is closer by arcsin(SPL)*(extra distance). Nearby means $|v| <= 4 * \text{SDev}/2$.

```
#define SPL .25881904514 /* sin(15 degrees): pay 15 degrees per unit distance */

real
Compatible(v, v1, v2)
vector  v, v1, v2;
{
    real        lengthv, sinv1v2;
    real        nearby_penalty;

    lengthv = v_norm(v);

    if (lengthv < 0.00000001 ||
        v_normsq(v1) == 0 || v_normsq(v2) == 0)
        return HUGE_PENALTY;  /* big penalty: same pixel! */

    sinv1v2 = fabs(v_dot(v_perp(v1), v2));
    nearby_penalty = sinv1v2 + SPL * lengthv;

    return nearby_penalty;
}
```

MergeCorners

Turns every CORNER that's not associated to a closed contour into a MIDDLE.

```
MergeCorners()
{
    Contour *c, *c1, *c2;
    ContourPoint *conpt;
    PixelInfo *p;
    int        end;
    int        merged;

    do {
        merged = FALSE;
        for (c = Contours; c != NULL; c = c->R) {
            c->split = FALSE;          /* automatic merge */

            for (end = 0; end <= 1; end++) {
                GetEnd(c, end, &conpt, &p);
                c1 = p->conpt[0].con;
                c2 = p->conpt[1].con;

                if (p->type == P_CORNER
                    && c1->closed == FALSE
                    && c2->closed == FALSE
                    /* both FALSE or both TRUE */
                    && c1->boundary == c2->boundary) {

                    /* Merge adds c2 to c1 and deletes c2 */
                    MergeCorner(p);
                    merged = TRUE; /* drop out; start w/1st contour */
                    break;
                }
            }
            if (merged)
                break;
        }
    } while (merged);
}
```

MergeCorner

Merges two contours by killing the corner at p, and deleting the second contour, p->conpt[1].con, from Contours. *Note: may reverse contours; may add closed contours.*

```
MergeCorner(p)
PixelInfo *p;
{
    PixelInfo *pt;
    ContourPoint *conpt;
    Contour *c1 = p->conpt[0].con;
    Contour *c2 = p->conpt[1].con;
    int         closed = FALSE;

    /* make p the tail of c1 and the head of c2 */
    GetEnd(c1, HEAD, &conpt, &pt);
    if (pt == p)
        ReverseContour(c1);

    GetEnd(c2, HEAD, &conpt, &pt);
    if (pt != p) {
        ReverseContour(c2);
        GetEnd(c2, HEAD, &conpt, &pt);
    }

    /* if the last point in c2 is p, build a closed contour */
    if (c1->end[HEAD].x == c2->end[TAIL].x &&
        c1->end[HEAD].y == c2->end[TAIL].y) {

        /* crazy case: c1 == c2 */
        if (c1->length == 2) {
            DeleteContour(c1);
            return;
        }
        if (c2->length == 2) {
            DeleteContour(c2);
            return;
        }

        /* just lop off the last point */
        LopOff(c2, TAIL, 1);
        closed = TRUE;
    }

    /* fetch 2nd point in c2 (1st point was the corner p) */
    GetNext(c2, FWD, &conpt, &pt);

    /* make p the middle of c1 */
    p->type = P_MIDDLE;
    p->conpt[0].n[FWD] = p->conpt[1].n[FWD];
    p->conpt[1].con = NULL;     /* null out the forward pointer in p */
    p->conpt[1].n[FWD] = 0;
    p->conpt[1].n[BACK] = 0;
```

```
/* change c2 contour pointers to c1 */
while (conpt != NULL) {
    conpt->con = c1;
    GetNext(c2, FWD, &conpt, &pt);
}
c1->length += (c2->length - 1);
c1->end[TAIL] = c2->end[TAIL];
c1->closed = closed;

/* and delete c2 from the list */
ExcludeContour(c2);
free(c2);                        /* why keep it around? */
NContours--;

/* don't leave a tiny closed contour */
if (c1->closed && c1->length < MIN_CLOSED)
    DeleteContour(c1);
}
```

GrowContours

Extends the end of each contour by reflecting successive points in a line perpendicular to the tangent near the endpoint. Connects if it runs into another contour before travelling maxgap from the end. If not, tries perturbing the angle of reflection a bit each way.

```
GrowContours(maxgap)
int       maxgap;
{
    Contour *c;
    int          changed;

    do {
        changed = FALSE;

        /* for each contour ... */
        for (c = Contours; c != NULL; c = c->R) {

            if (!c->closed && c->length >= maxgap)
                if (GrowContour(c, maxgap)) {
                    changed = TRUE;
                    break;
                }
        }
    } while (changed);
}
```

GrowContour

Extends each endpoint of a contour along a trajectory given by reflection in the line perpendicular to the contour's tangent near the endpoint. Connects if it runs into a contour within maxgap. If that fails, tries extending with the angle perturbed by +/-SweepAngle. Jumps directly to a corner if there is one within the trajectory.

```
GrowContour(c, maxgap)
Contour *c;
int      maxgap;
{
     ContourPoint *conpt;
     PixelInfo *p, *q;
     real        traj, reflectangle;
     real  si, co;
     int           end;

     /* for each of the two ends of the contour ... */
     for (end = 0; end <= 1; end++) {

          GetEnd(c, end, &conpt, &p);
          if (p->type != P_END)
               continue;

          /* use tangent by going in 4*SDev/2.0 from this end */
          q = NthFromEndP(c, end, IROUND(4*SDev / 3.0));
          if (q == NULL) {

               /* give it a second chance */
               q = NthFromEndP(c, end, IROUND(4*SDev / 4.0));
               if (q == NULL)
                    return FALSE;          /* not that long a contour */
          }

          traj = C_ANGLE(q, c);

          /* try going outward at  angle traj to find a corner */
          sincos(traj, &si, &co);          /* point traj away from q */
          if (si*(q->pos.y - p->pos.y)
              + co*(q->pos.x - p->pos.x) > 0)
               traj = MinusPiToPi(traj + M_PI);

          if (JumpToCorner(c, end, traj, maxgap * M_SQRT2))
               return TRUE;

          /* if not, grow by reflection */
          reflectangle = MinusPiToPi(traj + M_PI / 2.0);
          if (GrowEndpoint(c, end, maxgap, reflectangle))
               return TRUE;
```

```
          if (GrowEndpoint(c, end, maxgap,
                            MinusPiToPi(reflectangle + SweepAngle)))
               return TRUE;

          if (GrowEndpoint(c, end, maxgap,
                            MinusPiToPi(reflectangle - SweepAngle)))
               return TRUE;
     }
     return FALSE;
}


real
distance(x, y, x2, y2)
real    x, y, x2, y2;
{
     real       dx = x2 - x, dy = y2 - y;
     return sqrt(fabs(dx * dx + dy * dy));
}
```

Joinable

Returns a measure of how nice a candidate (x,y) to be joined to a contour. Zero means (x,y) is an impossible point to join to end end of con; 1 means (x,y) is an unused point (in PMap, has NULL or EMPTY pixelinfo), and n+1 means (x,y) runs into contours to which it could be joined, the longest of which is length n. If the contour to be joined is con itself, then n is the length of the longer of the two parts into which it would split if "joined."

```
int
Joinable(con, end, x, y)
Contour *con;
int       end;
int       x, y;
{
     int          i, n, n2;
     PixelInfo *p;

     if (x < 0 || x >= Width
         || y < 0 || y >= Height)
          return 0;

     if ((p = PMap[x][y]) == NULL || p->type == P_EMPTY)
          return 1;

     if (p->type == P_X)
              return 0;
```

```
        if (CONPT(p, con) != NO_CONTOUR) {

                /* p is a point on con */
                n = StepsToEnd(p, end, con);

                if (n <= TOO_SOON_TO_DOUBLE_BACK)
                        return 0;

                if (con->length - n > n)
                        n = con->length - n;
                n++;                            /* points = steps + 1 */
        } else {

                /* take largest stretch attached here */
                n = 0;
                for (i = 0; i < 4; i++)

                        if (p->conpt[i].con != NULL) {
                                n2 = p->conpt[i].con->length;

                                if (n2 > n)
                                        n = n2;
                        }
        }

        /* add 1 so it's always better than an empty point */
        return n + 1;
}
```

GrowEndPoint

Extends the end of a contour using a line-drawing routine to guarantee that the added points will all be 4-connected in the PMap. Checks nearest neighbors of each point added. Returns TRUE if it connects to another contour.

Note that there are shared variables for line drawing. This is less than elegant.

```
#define DEAD_END                  0
#define ADDED_NEW_POINT           1
#define JOINED_TO_SOMETHING       2

static Contour *__c;
static int __end;
static int *__Ppointno;
static real __reflectedangle;
static int __lastx, __lasty;
```

```
GrowEndpoint(c, end, maxgap, reflectangle)
Contour *c;
int      end;
int      maxgap;
real     reflectangle;
{
     ContourPoint *conpt, *stepinconpt;
     PixelInfo *stepin, *p;
     vector  endpoint;
     vector  from, to;                /* assure sequence of neighbors */
     PixelPos ifrom, ito;
     int          direction = (end == HEAD ? FWD : BACK);
     int          i, pointno, joined;
     int          AddBestNeighbor();

     GetEnd(c, end, &stepinconpt, &stepin);
     endpoint = stepin->pos;

     __c = c;
     __end = end;
     __Ppointno = &pointno;

     /* as we step inwards with stepin, reflect and add outwards */
     joined = FALSE;
     for (pointno = 0; pointno < maxgap;) {

          GetEnd(c, end, &conpt, &p);
          from = p->pos;
          ifrom = vectopp(from);
          GetNext(c, direction, &stepinconpt, &stepin);

          if (stepinconpt == NULL)/* ran out of points to reflect */
               break;

          /* find reflected point */
          to = Reflect(stepin->pos, endpoint, reflectangle);
          ito = vectopp(to);

          /* don't get carried away */
          if (ito.x < 0 || ito.x > Width - 1
              || ito.y < 0 || ito.y > Height - 1)
               break;

          if (ifrom.x == ito.x && ifrom.y == ito.y)
               continue;             /* just skip if we hit same pt twice */
```

```
                  /* Draw a line to the next point */
                  __reflectedangle = ReflectAngle(stepinconpt->angle,
                                                  reflectangle);
            i = ApplyToLineWhile(ifrom.x, ifrom.y,
                                 ito.x, ito.y,
                                 AddBestNeighbor,
                                 ADDED_NEW_POINT);

            if (i == DEAD_END)
                break;

            if (i == JOINED_TO_SOMETHING) {
                joined = TRUE;
                break;                  /* hit another contour */
            }
        }

        /* if we just grew but didn't join anything, shrink back */
        if (!joined && pointno > 0)
            LopOff(c, end, pointno);

        return joined;
}
```

AddBestNeighbor

Adds the most joinable neighbor of (x,y) (itself preferred) to contour c. This is called by the above function. All arguments besides x and y are all passed through externals to keep the line-drawing function fast. If it finds a more joinable neighbor than itself, adds itself first if necessary. Increments *(point counter) with each point added.

If (x,y) happens to be the end of the contour being grown, and there are no contours nearby to connect, fakes growing 1 point. This tells the line-drawing function to continue.

When choosing among equals, prefers the anti-neighbor of the contour endpoint if (x,y) itself is not in the running. Returns DEAD_END if no good neighbors were available, ADDED_NEW_POINT if it tacked a point or two on the end but didn't join up, or JOINED_TO_SOMETHING if joined up with something.

```
AddBestNeighbor(x, y)
int       x, y;
{
      int          ix, iy, bestdir, bestval, dir;
      int          val, joinability[NEIGHBORS];
      ContourPoint *conpt;
      PixelInfo *p;
      PixelPos pp;
      Contour *c = __c;
      int          *pn = __Ppointno;
      int          end = __end;
      int          dirConEndToXY;
```

```
bestval = 0;
for (dir = 0; dir < NEIGHBORS; dir++) {
    ix = x + NeighborPos[dir].x;
    iy = y + NeighborPos[dir].y;
    val = Joinable(c, end, ix, iy);
    joinability[dir] = val;

    if (val > bestval) {
        bestval = val;
        bestdir = dir;
    }
}

if (bestval == 0)
    return DEAD_END;

/* special case: are we trying to "add" the endpoint of c? */
if (bestval == 1 && c->end[end].x == x && c->end[end].y == y)
    return ADDED_NEW_POINT;          /* fake */

pp.x = x;
pp.y = y;
dirConEndToXY = WayToNhbr(c->end[end], pp);

/* prefer center if we have a choice */
if (bestval == joinability[0])
    bestdir = 0;

/* otherwise prefer antineighbor of endpoint */
else if (joinability[0] == 0
        && bestval == joinability[dirConEndToXY])
        bestdir = dirConEndToXY;
pp.x = x + NeighborPos[bestdir].x;
pp.y = y + NeighborPos[bestdir].y;

/* see if best neighbor is a direct neighbor of end end of contour c */
if (WayToNhbr(pp, c->end[end]) != 0) {
    if (AddPoint(c, end, (real) pp.x, (real) pp.y))
        return JOINED_TO_SOMETHING;
    goto NewPoint;
}

/* not direct neighbor, use x,y first */
if (bestdir == 0)
    /* this shouldn't happen */
    return DEAD_END;
```

```
    if (joinability[0] == 0)    /* x,y itself is not a good go-between */
        return DEAD_END;

    if (AddPoint(c, end, (real) x, (real) y))
        return JOINED_TO_SOMETHING;

    (*pn)++;
    GetEnd(c, end, &conpt, &p);
    conpt->angle = __reflectedangle;

    if (AddPoint(c, end, (real) pp.x, (real) pp.y))
        return JOINED_TO_SOMETHING;

 NewPoint:
    /* this is the new end, set its angle */
    GetEnd(c, end, &conpt, &p);
    conpt->angle = __reflectedangle;
    (*pn)++;
    return ADDED_NEW_POINT;
}

AddNeighbor(x, y) /* adds (x,y) to __c */
int      x, y;
{
    Contour *c = __c;
    int         *pn = __Ppointno;
    int          end = __end;

    /* special case: are we trying to add the endpoint of c? */
    if (c->end[end].x == x && c->end[end].y == y)
        return ADDED_NEW_POINT;        /* fake */

    if (AddPoint(c, end, (real) x, (real) y))
        return JOINED_TO_SOMETHING;
    (*pn)++;
    return ADDED_NEW_POINT;
}

CheckNeighbor(x, y) /* checks that (x,y) is clear */
int      x, y;
{
    Contour *c = __c;
    int          end = __end;
    PixelInfo *p;

    if (c->end[end].x == x && c->end[end].y == y)
        return ADDED_NEW_POINT;        /* fake */
```

```
    if ((p = PMap[x][y]) != NULL && p->type != P_EMPTY) {
        __lastx = x;
        __lasty = y;
        return JOINED_TO_SOMETHING;
    }
    return ADDED_NEW_POINT;
}
```

JumpToCorner

Checks all pixels within a cone radiating outward from the end of a given contour. If it
finds a CORNER, connects to it with the line drawing routine.

```
int
JumpToCorner(c, end, traj, dist)
Contour *c;
int      end;
real     traj;                         /* angle */
real     dist;                         /* max */
{
    int         left, right, bottom, top;
    real        x, y, distance();
    PixelInfo *p, *qbest;
    ContourPoint *conpt;
    int         AddNeighbor();

    /* cone: angle traj+/-SweepAngle, radius between 0 and dist */
    GetEnd(c, end, &conpt, &p);
    left = right = IROUND(p->pos.x);
    bottom = top = IROUND(p->pos.y);

    /* get bounding box of cone */
    x = IROUND(p->pos.x + dist * cos(traj - SweepAngle));
    y = IROUND(p->pos.y + dist * sin(traj - SweepAngle));

    if (x < 0) x = 0;
    if (x > Width - 1) x = Width - 1;
    if (y < 0) y = 0;
    if (y > Height - 1) y = Height - 1;

    if (left > x) left = x;
    if (right < x) right = x;
    if (bottom > y) bottom = y;
    if (top < y) top = y;

    x = IROUND(p->pos.x + dist * cos(traj + SweepAngle));
    y = IROUND(p->pos.y + dist * sin(traj + SweepAngle));
```

```
if (x < 0) x = 0;
if (x > Width - 1) x = Width - 1;
if (y < 0) y = 0;
if (y > Height - 1) y = Height - 1;

if (left > x) left = x;
if (right < x) right = x;
if (bottom > y) bottom = y;
if (top < y) top = y;

/* look for corners therein */
qbest = NULL;
for (y = bottom; y <= top; y++) {

    for (x = left; x <= right; x++) {
        real      theta;
        PixelInfo *q;

        if (y == p->pos.y && x == p->pos.x)
            continue;

        q = PMap[IROUND(x)][IROUND(y)];
        if (q == NULL || q->type != P_CORNER)
            continue;

        theta = MinusPiToPi(atan2(y-p->pos.y, x-p->pos.x));
        if (theta < traj - SweepAngle
            || theta > traj + SweepAngle)
            continue;

        /* verify that the line draws without intercepts */
        __c = c;
        __end = end;
        ApplyToLineWhile(IROUND(p->pos.x), IROUND(p->pos.y),
                         IROUND(q->pos.x), IROUND(q->pos.y),
                         CheckNeighbor,
                         ADDED_NEW_POINT);

        if (__lastx != IROUND(q->pos.x)
            || __lasty != IROUND(q->pos.y))
            continue;

        if (qbest == NULL
            || distance(p->pos.x, p->pos.y,
                        q->pos.x, q->pos.y)
             < distance(p->pos.x, p->pos.y,
                        qbest->pos.x, qbest->pos.y))
            qbest = q;
    }
}
```

```
    if (qbest != NULL) {
        int     pno = 0;
        /* connect with a straight line! */
        __c = c;
        __end = end;
        __Ppointno = &pno;

        ApplyToLineWhile(IROUND(p->pos.x), IROUND(p->pos.y),
                         IROUND(qbest->pos.x),
                         IROUND(qbest->pos.y),
                         AddNeighbor,
                         ADDED_NEW_POINT);
        return TRUE;
    }
    return FALSE;
}
```

Point lists for simple storage of contours

```
typedef struct PointList {
    int         n;                          /* points in each array */
    real    *x, *y, *tan, *k, *L;           /* L is for cornerness */
} PointList;


PointList *BuildPointList(Contour *con);  /* alloc, fill new PointList */
```

FindCorners

Finds local maxima of Cornerness >= thresh along contours. Only one is allowed
per neighborhood of radius r. Ends of contours do not count as corners.

```
FindCorners(thresh, r)
real    thresh, r;
{
    int         changed;
    int         nfound = 0;
    Contour *c;

    do {
        changed = FALSE;

        for (c = Contours; c != NULL; c = c->R) {
            PointList *plist = BuildPointList(c);
            int     n = c->length;
            int     i;
```

```
                              /* any pixel that is best in the nbhd */
                              for (i = 0; i < n; i++) {
                                      /* mark c as not closed if it has a corner near an endpoint */
                                      if (CornerLocalMax(plist, i, thresh, r,
                                                         c->closed && !c->split)) {

                                              /* got one */
                                              SplitContour(c, NthFromEndP(c, HEAD, i));
                                              changed = TRUE;
                                              nfound++;
                                              break;
                                      }
                              }
                              FreePointList(plist);

                              if (changed)
                                      break;
                      }
              } while (changed);
      }

PDist(plist, i, j)            /* distance between points in a PointList */
PointList *plist;
int       i, j;
{
      real dx = plist->x[j] - plist->x[i];
      real dy = plist->y[j] - plist->y[i];

      if (dx == 0 && dy == 0)
            return 0;
      return sqrt(fabs(dx * dx + dy * dy));
}
```

CornerLocalMax

Returns TRUE if cornerness is a local max at point i. Compares back and forth, wrapping if closed. If not closed, then disqualifies if point i is too near either end.

```
CornerLocalMax(plist, i, thresh, r, closed)
PointList *plist;
int       i;
real      thresh, r;
int       closed;
{
      int          j;
      int          n = plist->n;
```

```
/* must be above thresh */
if (plist->L[i] < thresh)
    return FALSE;


if (!closed) {

    /* within r of either end ? */
    if (PDist(plist, 0, i) < r || PDist(plist, n - 1, i) < r)
        return FALSE;
}


/* must be local max within the nbhd */
for (j = i + 1;; j++) {

    if (closed && j > n - 1)
        j -= n;
    if (j == i || j > n - 1)
        break;

    if (PDist(plist, i, j) >= r)
        break;

    /* finally, check if a neighbor has stronger cornerness */
    if (plist->L[i] < plist->L[j])
        return FALSE;
}

for (j = i - 1;; j--) {

    if (closed && j < 0)
        j += n;
    if (j == i || j < 0)
        break;

    if (PDist(plist, i, j) >= r)
        break;

    if (plist->L[i] < plist->L[j])
        return FALSE;
}
return TRUE;
}
```

Delete...

These functions prune contours that fall short of certain criteria.

```
DeleteShort(length)
int      length;
{
     Contour *c, *next;

     for (c = Contours; c != NULL; c = next) {
          next = c->R;

          if (!c->boundary && c->length < length) {
               DeleteContour(c);
          }
     }
}

DeleteUntethered(length)
int      length;
{
     Contour *c, *next;
     ContourPoint *conpt;
     PixelInfo *p, *q;

     for (c = Contours; c != NULL; c = next) {
          next = c->R;

          if (!c->boundary && c->length < length) {
               GetEnd(c, HEAD, &conpt, &p);
               GetEnd(c, TAIL, &conpt, &q);

               if (p->type == P_POINT ||
                   (p->type == P_END && q->type == P_END))
                    DeleteContour(c);
          }
     }
}

DeleteStray(min)
int      min;
{
     Contour *c, *next;
     ContourPoint *conpt;
     PixelInfo *p;
     int          end;
     int          changed;
     int          i, j, nothers;
     int          hitboundary;
     Contour *others[6];
```

```
do {
    changed = FALSE;
    DeleteUntethered(min);
    MergeCorners();

    for (c = Contours; c != NULL; c = next) {
        next = c->R;

        if (c->boundary)
            continue;

        if (!c->closed) {
            for (end = 0; end <= 1; end++) {
                GetEnd(c, end, &conpt, &p);

                if (p->type==P_END
                    || p->type==P_POINT) {
                    DeleteContour(c);
                    changed = TRUE;
                    break;      /* to outer loop */
                }
            }
        }

        /* delete if connected to only 1 other contour */
        if (changed)
            break;
        if (c->length >= min)
            continue;

        /* count other contours to which it is connected */
        /* (count image boundary only once) */
        nothers = 0;
        hitboundary = FALSE;
        for (end = 0; end <= 1; end++) {
            GetEnd(c, end, &conpt, &p);

            for (i = 0; i < 4; i++) {
                Contour *c2 = p->conpt[i].con;

                if (c2 != NULL && c2 != c) {

                    /* only 1st of image border */
                    if (c2->boundary) {
                        if (hitboundary)
                            break;
                        hitboundary = TRUE;
                    }
```

```
                                        for (j = 0; j < nothers; j++)
                                            if (c2 == others[j])
                                                break;

                                        /* connected to somebody else */
                                        if (j >= nothers)
                                            others[nothers++] = c2;
                                }
                        }
                }

                if (nothers <= 1) {
                        DeleteContour(c);
                        changed = TRUE;
                        break;
                }
        }
    } while (changed);
}

DeleteContour(c)
Contour *c;
{
    LopOff(c, HEAD, c->length);
    ExcludeContour(c);
    free(c);
    NContours--;
}

LopOff(c, end, npoints) /* kill n points from c starting at end */
Contour *c;
int     end;
int     npoints;
{
    ContourPoint *conpt, *nextconpt;
    PixelInfo *p, *nextp;
    PixelType oldtype;
    int         direction = (end == HEAD ? FWD : BACK);
    int         lopped;

    if (npoints == 0)
        return;

    /* leave pointers to this contour */
    for (lopped = 0, GetEnd(c, end, &conpt, &p);
        conpt != NULL && lopped < npoints; lopped++) {
```

```
/* find next ones */
nextconpt = conpt;
nextp = p;
oldtype = p->type;
GetNext(c, direction, &nextconpt, &nextp);

switch (p->type) {

case P_EMPTY:              /* not on any contour */
     break;                /* nothing to do */

case P_POINT:
case P_END:
case P_MIDDLE:
     p->type = P_EMPTY;
     break;

case P_CORNER:             /* 2 con's end here, different tangents */
     p->type = P_END;

     /* shift */
     if (p->conpt[0].con == c)
         p->conpt[0] = p->conpt[1];

     conpt = &p->conpt[1];      /* to be nulled */
     break;

case P_T:                  /* triple -> corner, even if it shouldn't */
case P_Y:
     p->type = P_CORNER;

     if (p->conpt[0].con == c) {
         p->conpt[0] = p->conpt[1];
         p->conpt[1] = p->conpt[2];
     } else if (p->conpt[1].con == c) {
         p->conpt[1] = p->conpt[2];
     }
     conpt = &p->conpt[2];      /* to be nulled */
     break;

case P_X:                  /* 4 contours -> triple */
     p->type = P_Y;
```

```
            if (p->conpt[0].con == c) {
                p->conpt[0] = p->conpt[1];
                p->conpt[1] = p->conpt[2];
                p->conpt[2] = p->conpt[3];
            } else if (p->conpt[1].con == c) {
                p->conpt[1] = p->conpt[2];
                p->conpt[2] = p->conpt[3];
            } else if (p->conpt[2].con == c) {
                p->conpt[2] = p->conpt[3];
            }
            conpt = &p->conpt[3];      /* to be nulled */
            break;
        }

        /* null out the now-unused contour point */
        conpt->n[0] = conpt->n[1] = 0;
        conpt->con = NULL;
        conpt->angle = 0.0;

        /* bump the "end" up to the next point, if there is one */
        if (nextconpt != NULL) {
            nextconpt->n[direction == FWD ?
                        BACK : FWD] = 0;
            c->end[end].x = IROUND(nextp->pos.x);
            c->end[end].y = IROUND(nextp->pos.y);

            if (nextp->type == P_MIDDLE)
                nextp->type = P_END;
            else if (nextp->type == P_END)
                nextp->type = P_POINT;
        }
        c->length--;

        /* set p and conpt to next */
        conpt = nextconpt;
        p = nextp;
    }
    c->closed = FALSE;              /* not closed any more! */

    /* make sure we're not leaving a trivial contour at a multiple-point */
    if (nextconpt != NULL && c->length == 1
        && nextp->type != P_POINT) {
        warn("Lopped off all but stub of contour.\n");
    }
}
```

```
ExcludeContour(c)  /* remove c from Contours */
Contour *c;
{
    Contour *prev;

    if (Contours == NULL)
        return;

    if (c == Contours) {
        Contours = Contours->R;
        return;
    }

    for (prev = Contours; prev->R != NULL && prev->R != c;)
        prev = prev->R;
    prev->R = c->R;
}

ReverseContour(c)  /* reverse order of ContourPoints in c */
Contour *c;
{
    ContourPoint *conpt;
    PixelInfo *p;
    PixelPos postemp;
    int         temp;

    GetEnd(c, HEAD, &conpt, &p);

    /* switch head and tail */
    postemp = c->end[HEAD];
    c->end[HEAD] = c->end[TAIL];
    c->end[TAIL] = postemp;

    /* switch n[FWD] with n[BACK] and reverse theta */
    do {
        /* stash the next one */
        temp = conpt->n[FWD];
        conpt->n[FWD] = conpt->n[BACK];
        conpt->n[BACK] = temp;
        conpt->angle = MinusPiToPi(conpt->angle + M_PI);

        /* bump forward (remember we switched) */
        GetNext(c, BACK, &conpt, &p);
    } while (conpt != NULL);
}
```

SplitContour

Splits a contour from its HEAD up to and including a given cutting point, making a new contour structure, which is placed at the beginning of the Contours list. The original contour is truncated to start at the split point, which now becomes a CORNER, and continues to the original TAIL. Assumes contour points besides head and tail are all of type MIDDLE.

```
SplitContour(c, cutp)
Contour *c;
PixelInfo *cutp;
{
    Contour *newcon;
    ContourPoint *head, *tail, *cutpoint, *startpoint;
    int          length, origlength = c->length;
    PixelPos pos;
    PixelInfo *p, *q;
    int          tailmatch;

    pos = vectopp(cutp->pos);
    cutpoint = &cutp->conpt[0];

    if (c->closed &&
        ((pos.x == c->end[HEAD].x && pos.y == c->end[HEAD].y)
         || (tailmatch = (pos.x == c->end[TAIL].x
                          && pos.y == c->end[TAIL].y)))) {
        if (!FirstPass)
            c->split = TRUE;

        /* assure that cut point is at head */
        if (tailmatch)
            ReverseContour(c);
        return;
    }

    /* get head and tail */
    GetEnd(c, HEAD, &head, &p);
    GetEnd(c, TAIL, &tail, &q);

    if (c->closed && !c->split
        && p->type == P_END && q->type == P_END) {
        ContourPoint *cutpoint1;
        PixelInfo *cutp1;

        p->type = P_MIDDLE;
        q->type = P_MIDDLE;
        p->conpt[0].n[BACK] = WayToNhbr(c->end[HEAD],
                                        c->end[TAIL]);
        q->conpt[0].n[FWD] = AntiNhbr[p->conpt[0].n[BACK]];
```

```
    /* make cutp new head and cutp1 (next backward) new tail */
    cutp1 = cutp;
    cutpoint1 = cutpoint;
    GetNext(c, BACK, &cutpoint1, &cutp1);
    cutp->type = P_END;
    cutp->conpt[0].n[BACK] = 0;

    c->end[HEAD] = vectopp(cutp->pos);
    cutp1->type = P_END;
    cutp1->conpt[0].n[FWD] = 0;
    c->end[TAIL] = vectopp(cutp1->pos);

    /* make a note that it was deliberately split there */
    if (!FirstPass)
        c->split = TRUE;
    return;
}

/* passed the test - make a new contour structure and add to list */
newcon = NewContour(pos.x, pos.y);
newcon->end[HEAD] = c->end[HEAD];
newcon->end[TAIL] = pos;    /* this was already done by NewContour */
newcon->boundary = c->boundary;       /* boundary contour splits */

/* bump head up to cutpoint, changing contour pointers to newcon */
length = 0;
for (;;) {
    head->con = newcon;
    length++;

    if (head == cutpoint)
        break;
    GetNext(c, FWD, &head, &p);
}

cutp->type = P_CORNER;
/* take the next contour point slot */
startpoint = &cutp->conpt[1];
startpoint->con = c;
startpoint->angle = cutpoint->angle; /* so why is it a corner? */
startpoint->n[FWD] = cutpoint->n[FWD];
cutpoint->n[FWD] = 0;

/* change HEAD of the original contour to the cutpoint */
c->end[HEAD] = vectopp(cutp->pos);
newcon->length = length;
c->length = origlength - length + 1; /* count cutpoint twice */
```

```
        if (c->closed) {
            c->closed = FALSE;

            if (PMap[newcon->end[HEAD].x][newcon->end[HEAD].y]->type
                    == P_END)
                AddPoint(newcon, HEAD,
                        (real) c->end[TAIL].x,
                        (real) c->end[TAIL].y);

            else if (PMap[c->end[TAIL].x][c->end[TAIL].y]->type
                    == P_END)
                AddPoint(c, TAIL,
                        (real) newcon->end[HEAD].x,
                        (real) newcon->end[HEAD].y);
        }
        c->closed = FALSE;
        c->split = FALSE;
}
```

JoinContour

Joining two contours into one is just a bookkeeping task.

```
JoinContour(c, end, p)
Contour *c;
int       end;
PixelInfo *p;
{
        PixelPos pos;
        ContourPoint *endconpt, *conpt;
        PixelInfo *endp;
        Contour *ac;
        int         dir;                /* neighbor direction from p to end of c */

        pos.x = IROUND(p->pos.x);
        pos.y = IROUND(p->pos.y);
        dir = WayToNhbr(pos, c->end[end]);

        /* get end pixel and conpt */
        GetEnd(c, end, &endconpt, &endp);

        /* make sure we're not joining p to p */
        if (p == endp)
            return;

        /* attach to p according to type */
        switch (p->type) {
```

```
case P_EMPTY:                         /* not on any contour--just add to head */
    p->type = P_END;
    conpt = &p->conpt[0];
    break;

case P_POINT:                         /* attach to trivial contour */
    conpt = &p->conpt[0];
    DeleteContour(conpt->con);        /* don't leave bits around! */

    /* remember Delete turns p from POINT into EMPTY */
    p->type = P_END;
    break;

case P_END:                           /* another contour ends here--corner */
    if (p->conpt[0].con == c) {

        /* just ran into its own tail */
        if (c->length >= MIN_CLOSED)
            c->closed = TRUE;
        return;
    }
    p->type = P_CORNER;
    conpt = &p->conpt[1];
    break;

case P_MIDDLE:        /* end of contour runs into middle of another */
    if (p->conpt[0].con == c) {

        /* ran into self! Split c at p by turning it into a corner */
        SplitContour(c, p);
        if (p->type != P_CORNER) {
            /* ?closed? contour ran into its own middle */
            return;
        }

        /* mark the contour that goes from c's old end to p as closed */
        if (end == HEAD)
            ac = p->conpt[0].con;
        else
            ac = p->conpt[1].con;

        if (ac->length >= MIN_CLOSED)
            ac->closed = TRUE;
        return;
    }

    /* split into P_CORNER and then turn into Y */
    SplitContour(p->conpt[0].con, p);
    if (p->type == P_END) {
```

```
                     /* splitting simple closed contour just shuffles ends around */
                     p->type = P_CORNER;
                     conpt = &p->conpt[1];
                     break;
             }
             p->type = P_Y;
             conpt = &p->conpt[2];
             break;

     case P_CORNER:        /* 2 contours end here, diff angles, becomes a Y */
             if (p->conpt[0].con == c || p->conpt[1].con == c) {

                     /* c ran into its own other end */
                     if (c->length >= MIN_CLOSED)
                             c->closed = TRUE;
                     return;
             }
             p->type = P_Y;
             conpt = &p->conpt[2];
             break;

     case P_T:                     /* 3 contours end here – turn into P_X */
     case P_Y:
             if (p->conpt[0].con == c || p->conpt[1].con == c
                 || p->conpt[2].con == c) {

                     /* highly unlikely: a three-leaf clover? */
                     if (c->length >= MIN_CLOSED)
                             c->closed = TRUE;
                     return;
             }
             p->type = P_X;
             conpt = &p->conpt[3];
             break;

     case P_X:                     /* 4 contours end here, 2 pairs of matching tangents */
             /* can't join */
             return;
     }

     /* update the old end point info */
     if (endp->type == P_POINT)
             endp->type = P_END;
     else if (endp->type == P_END)
             endp->type = P_MIDDLE;
     else                                  /* two neighboring corners or Y's? */
             assert(0);       /* fail */
```

```
    /* pointers */
    conpt->con = c;
    conpt->n[end == HEAD ? FWD : BACK] = dir;   /* from p to old end */
    endconpt->n[end == HEAD ? BACK : FWD] = AntiNhbr[dir];
    c->end[end] = pos;            /* p is c's new end */
    c->length++;

    if (FirstPass && p->type == P_CORNER)
        MergeCorner(p);
}
```

Support functions ...

```
real
MinusPiToPi(a)   /* give an equivalent angle between −π and π */
real    a;
{
    while (a > M_PI)
        a -= 2 * M_PI;

    while (a < -M_PI)
        a += 2 * M_PI;

    return a;
}

StepsToEnd(pcand, end, con)          /* points from here to end of con */
PixelInfo *pcand;
int       end;
Contour *con;
{
    ContourPoint *conpt;
    PixelInfo *p;
    int          direction = (end == HEAD ? FWD : BACK);
    int          nsteps;

    nsteps = 0;
    for (GetEnd(con, end, &conpt, &p); conpt != NULL;
        GetNext(con, direction, &conpt, &p)) {

        if (p == pcand)
            break;
        nsteps++;
    }

    if (p != pcand)
        return 10000; /* candidate wasn't part of con! */
    return nsteps;
}
```

```
vector
Reflect(p, nail, nailtheta)          /* reflects p in the given line */
vector   p, nail;
real     nailtheta;
{
     real       sint, cost;
     vector  result, v, w;

     sincos(2.0 * nailtheta, &sint, &cost);
     v = v_difference(nail, p); /* v = (p-nail) */

     /* w = matrix(cost sint / sint -cost).v */
     w.x = cost * v.x + sint * v.y;
     w.y = sint * v.x - cost * v.y;
     result = v_sum(w, nail); /* w + nail */
     return result;
}


real
ReflectAngle(theta, axisangle)
real     theta, axisangle;
{
     return MinusPiToPi(2.0 * (axisangle) - (theta));
}


int
WayToNhbr(p1, p2)              /* direction (1..8) to get from p1 to p2 */
PixelPos p1, p2;
{
     PixelPos diff;
     int          n;

     diff.y = p2.y - p1.y;
     diff.x = p2.x - p1.x;
     for (n = 0; n < NEIGHBORS; n++)

          if (diff.x == NeighborPos[n].x
              && diff.y == NeighborPos[n].y)
               return n;

     /* non-neighbors */
     return 0;
}
```

```
PixelInfo *
NthFromEndP(c, end, npix)            /* pth point along c from end */
Contour *c;
int      end;
int      npix;
{
     PixelInfo *p;
     ContourPoint *conpt;
     int            direction = (end == HEAD ? FWD : BACK);

     GetEnd(c, end, &conpt, &p);
     while (npix-- > 0 && conpt != NULL)
          GetNext(c, direction, &conpt, &p);

     if (conpt == NULL)
          return NULL;

     return p;
}
```

Walking along contours

Start a walk along a contour in the pixel map.

```
GetEnd(con, whichend, conpt, pixinfo)
Contour *con;
int      whichend;
ContourPoint **conpt;
PixelInfo **pixinfo;
{
     PixelInfo *p;
     p = PMap[con->end[whichend].x][con->end[whichend].y];
     *conpt = &p->conpt[CONPT_force(p, con)];
     *pixinfo = p;
}
```

Continue a walk along a contour in the pixel map.

```
GetNext(con, direction, conpt, pixinfo)
Contour *con;
int      direction;
ContourPoint **conpt;
PixelInfo **pixinfo;
{
     int           dir;
     PixelInfo *p;
```

```
        dir = (*conpt)->n[direction];
        if (dir == 0) {
            *conpt = NULL;
            return;
        }

        p = *pixinfo;
        p = PMap(NeighborPos[dir].x + IROUND(p->pos.x),
                 NeighborPos[dir].y + IROUND(p->pos.y));
        *conpt = &p->conpt[CONPT_force(p, con)];
        *pixinfo = p;
}
```

Line-drawing

ApplyToLineWhile calls a given function f(x,y) for all grid points on an approximate
line. If at any point f() returns anything but val, aborts and returns the value that f()
returned. Returns val for success.

```
#define SGN(x)              ((x)<0 ? -1 : 1)


int
ApplyToLineWhile(fromx, fromy, tox, toy, f, val)
int       fromx, fromy, tox, toy, val;
int       (*f) ();
{
      int         x, y, dx, dy, flipxy, retval;
      int         xinc, yinc, incr1, incr2, d, xmin, xmax;
      int         npoints;

      dx = ABS(fromx - tox);
      dy = ABS(fromy - toy);
      if (dx == 0 && dy == 0) {
          return val;
      }

      if (dy < dx) {
          /* iterate x, and then sometimes y */
          flipxy = FALSE;

          /* initialize */
          d = (2 * dy) - dx;       /* "divergence" from line */
          incr1 = 2 * dy;                   /* increment if d < 0 */
          incr2 = 2 * (dy - dx);            /* increment if d >= 0 */
```

```
        /* x moves from from to to, y according to slope */
        xinc = SGN(tox - fromx);
        yinc = xinc * SGN((toy - fromy) * (tox - fromx));
        x = fromx;
        y = fromy;
        xmin = MIN(fromx, tox);
        xmax = MAX(fromx, tox);
    } else {
        /* above code with fromx/y, tox/y, and dx/y flipped */
        flipxy = TRUE;

        /* initialize */
        d = (2 * dx) - dy;      /* "divergence" from line */
        incr1 = 2 * dx;                   /* increment if d < 0 */
        incr2 = 2 * (dx - dy);            /* increment if d >= 0 */

        /* x moves from from to to, y according to slope */
        xinc = SGN(toy - fromy);
        yinc = xinc * SGN((tox - fromx) * (toy - fromy));
        x = fromy;
        y = fromx;
        xmin = MIN(fromy, toy);
        xmax = MAX(fromy, toy);
    }

    /* draw first point */
    retval = (flipxy ? (*f) (y, x) : (*f) (x, y));
    if (retval != val)
        return retval;

    for (npoints = 0;; npoints++) {
        x += xinc;

        if (d < 0)
            d += incr1;
        else {
            y += yinc;
            d += incr2;
        }

        if (x < xmin || x > xmax)
            break;

        retval = (flipxy ? (*f) (y, x) : (*f) (x, y));
        if (retval != val)
            return retval;
    }
    return val;
}
```

Storage management

```
PixelInfo *
NewPixelInfo(x, y)          /* put new structure at PMap[x][y] */
int     x, y;
{
    PixelInfo *p;
    real        cos, sin;

    p = (PixelInfo *) calloc(sizeof (PixelInfo), 1);
    p->type = P_EMPTY;
    p->pos = v_vec((real) x, (real) y);
    p->k = 0;
    cos = Edgex[x][y];
    sin = Edgey[x][y];

    if (cos != 0 || sin != 0)
        p->conpt[0].angle = atan2(sin, cos);
    else
        p->conpt[0].angle = 0;

    NPixelInfos++;
    return p;
}

Contour *
NewContour(x, y)            /* new member of Contours; 1 pt (x,y) */
int     x, y;
{
    Contour *con;
    PixelInfo *pixelinfo;

    con = (Contour *) calloc(sizeof (Contour), 1);
    con->end[HEAD].x = x;
    con->end[HEAD].y = y;
    con->end[TAIL].x = x;
    con->end[TAIL].y = y;
    con->length = 1;
    con->closed = FALSE;        /* not a closed curve */
    con->split = FALSE;         /* not a kinked closed curve */
    con->boundary = FALSE;      /* not on image border */

    if (PMap[x][y] == NULL) {
        pixelinfo = PMap[x][y] = NewPixelInfo(x, y);
        pixelinfo->type = P_POINT;
        pixelinfo->conpt[0].con = con;
        /* conpt[i].n[j] all i,j "next" pointers are 0 */
    }
```

```
    /* else the caller must take care of that */
    con->R = Contours;
    Contours = con;
    NContours++;
    return con;
}
```

DrawBorder

Builds a closed contour that is the border of the image pad pixels in from the actual image boundary.

```
DrawBorder(pad)
int       pad;
{
    Contour *c, *NewContour();
    real        x, y;

    x = pad;
    y = pad;
    c = NewContour(x, y);
    c->boundary = TRUE;                        /* image boundary */

    for (x++; x < Width - pad; x++)
        AddPoint(c, HEAD, x, y);
    for (x--, y++; y < Height - pad; y++)
        AddPoint(c, HEAD, x, y);
    for (y--, x--; x >= pad; x--)
        AddPoint(c, HEAD, x, y);
    for (x++, y--; y >= pad; y--)
        AddPoint(c, HEAD, x, y);
}
```

Bibliography

[1] D. Beymer, Massachusetts Institute of Technology Master's thesis, *Junctions: Their detection and use for grouping in images*, 1989.

[2] Bitstream, Inc., Cambridge, Massachusetts. A proprietary interactive font input system launched this digital font supplier in 1981.

[3] A. Blake and A. Zisserman, *Using Weak Continuity Constraints*, Report CSR-186-85, Department of Computer Science, Edinburgh University, 1985.

[4] R. Bryant, and P. Griffiths, "Reduction for constrained variational problems and $\int \frac{\kappa^2}{2} ds$". *Amer. J. Math.*, **108** (1986), p. 525.

[5] J. Canny, *Finding Edges and Lines in Images*, MIT AI Technical Report No. 720, June 1983.

[6] P. Cavanaugh, "What's up in top-down processing?" In A. Gorea, ed. *Representations of Vision: Trends and Tacit Assumptions in Vision Research*, Cambridge, UK: Cambridge University Press, 1991, pp.295–304.

[7] C. David and S. Zucker, *Potentials, Valleys, and Dynamic Global Coverings*, McGill University Technical Report TR-CIM 89-1, March 1989.

[8] L. Euler, *Methodus inveniendi lineas curvas maximi minimive proprietate gaudentes*, Lausanne, 1744.

[9] B. Flannery, W. H. Press, S. A. Teukolsky and W. T. Vetterling, *Numerical Recipes in C*, Cambridge University Press, Cambridge, 1988.

[10] W. Freeman, "Steerable Filters and Local Analysis of Image Structure," PhD Thesis, Massachusetts Institute of Technology, Cambridge, Mass., 1992.

[11] W. Freeman and T. Adelson, "Steerable Filters," *Proceedings of the Third International Conference on Computer Vision*, Osaka, 1990.

[12] S. Geman and D. Geman, *Stochastic Relaxation, Gibbs Distribution, and the Bayesian Restoration of Images*, IEEE Trans., PAMI 6, pp.721–741, 1984.

[13] R. Graham, "Snow removal: A noise-stripping process for TV signals," *IRE Trans. Information Theory* **IT-8**, 129-144, (1962).

[14] A. Guzman, "Decomposition of a visual scene into three-dimensional bodies," in *AFIPS Conf. Proc.* **33**, 291-304 (1968).

[15] R. von der Heydt, E. Peterhans and G. Baumgartner, "Illusory Contours and Cortical Neuron Responses," *Science* **224** 1260-1262, 1984.

[16] B. Julesz, *The Foundations of Cyclopean Perception*, Chicago University Press, Chicago, 1971.

[17] G. Kanizsa, *Organization in Vision*, New York: Praeger, 1979, Ch. 1-2.

[18] P. Kellman, and T. Shipley, "Visual Interpolation in Object Perception: A Computational Theory", manuscript, Swarthmore College, April 1990.

[19] L. Kitchen and A. Rosenfeld, *Gray-Level Corner Detection*, Technical Report TR-887, Computer Science Center, University of Maryland, College Park, 1980.

[20] A. Lev, S. Zucker and A. Rosenfeld, "Iterative Enhancement of Noisy Images," *IEEE Trans. on Systems, Man and Cybernetics* **SMC-7**, 435-442 (1977).

[21] A. Love, *A treatise on the mathematical theory of elasticity*, Cambridge: The University Press, 1934.

[22] D. Lowe, "Organization of Smooth Image Curves at Multiple Scales," *Proceedings of the Second International Conference on Computer Vision*, 1988, pp. 558-567.

[23] D. Marr and E. Hildreth, "Theory of edge detection," *Proc. R. Soc. Lond. B* **207** (1980) 269-294.

[24] D. Marr, *Vision*, New York: W H Freeman and Company, 1982.

[25] J. Marroquin, *Surface Reconstruction Preserving Discontinuities*, A.I. Lab. Memo No. 792, MIT, 1984.

[26] D. Mumford, "Elastica and Computer Vision," in *Algebraic Geometry and Applications*, C. Bajaj, ed., Heidelberg: Springer-Verlag, 1992.

[27] D. Mumford, "The Computational Architecture of the Neocortex," manuscript, Harvard University, November 1990.

[28] D. Mumford, and J. Shah, "Optimal Approximations of Piecewise Smooth Functions and Associated Variational Problems", *Comm. in Pure and Appl. Math.*, 1989, **42**, pp.577-685.

[29] M. Nagao and T. Matsuyama, "Edge Preserving Smoothing," *Computer Graphics and Image Processing* **9**, 394-407 (1979).

[30] H. Nagel, "Displacement Vectors Derived from Second-Order Intensity Variations in Image Sequences," *Computer Vision, Graphics, and Image Processing* **21**, 85-117 (1983).

[31] K. Nakayama and S. Shimojo, "Da Vinci stereopsis: depth and subjective occluding contours from unpaired image points," *Vision Research* **30** 1811-1825 (1990).

[32] K. Nakayama and S. Shimojo, "Towards a neural understanding of visual surface representation," *Cold Spring Harbor Symposium on Quantitative Biology*, Volume 55, The Brain, Edited by T. Sejnowski, E. R. Kandel, C. F. Stevens and J. D. Watson, 1990.

[33] T. G. Newman and H. Dirilten, "A nonlinear transformation for digital picture processing," *IEEE Trans. Computers* **C-22** 869-873, (1973).

[34] M. Nitzberg and D. Mumford, "The 2.1-D Sketch", in *Proceedings of the Third International Conference on Computer Vision*, Osaka, 1990.

[35] M. Nitzberg and T. Shiota, *Nonlinear Smoothing with Edge and Corner Enhancement* Harvard Robotics Laboratory Technical Report No. 90-2, Harvard University, April 1990.

[36] M. Paradiso, S. Shimojo and K. Nakayama, "Subjective contours, tilt aftereffects and visual cortical organization," *Vision Research* **29** 1205-1213 (1989).

[37] P. Perona and J. Malik, "Scale-Space and Edge Detection Using Anisotropic Diffusion," *IEEE Trans. on Pat. Anal. Mach. Intell.* **PAMI-12** 629-639 (July 1990).

[38] P. Perona, "Steerable-Scalable Kernels for Edge Detection and Junction Analysis," in Lecture Notes in Computer Science, Vol. 588, *Computer Vision – ECCV '92*, G. Sandini (Ed.), Heidelberg: Springer Verlag, 1992.

[39] L. Roberts, "Machine perception of three-dimensional solids," in *Optical and electro optical information processing*, ed. J. Tippett et al., 159-197, MIT Press, Cambridge, Mass., 1965.

[40] L. Rosenthaller, F. Heitger, O. Kübler, and R. von der Heydt, "Detection of General Edges and Keypoints," in Lecture Notes in Computer Science, Vol. 588, *Computer Vision – ECCV '92*, G. Sandini (Ed.), Heidelberg: Springer Verlag, 1992.

[41] S. Shimojo and K. Nakayama, "Amodal representation of occluded surfaces: role of invisible stimuli in apparent motion correspondence," *Perception* **19**, 285-299 (1990).

[42] L. Williams, "Perceptual organization of occluding contours," in *Proceedings of the Third International Conference on Computer Vision*, Osaka, 1990.

[43] G. Xu and S. Tsuji, "Object Recognition and Learning: 3-Dimensional or 2-Dimensional?" Osaka University Dept. of Control Engineering Technical Report 91-01, January 1991.

[44] S. Zucker, R. Hummel and A. Rosenfeld, "An application of relaxation labeling to line and curve enhancement," *IEEE Transactions on Computers* **26** (1977).

Springer-Verlag
and the Environment

$\mathbf{W}$e at Springer-Verlag firmly believe that an international science publisher has a special obligation to the environment, and our corporate policies consistently reflect this conviction.

$\mathbf{W}$e also expect our business partners – paper mills, printers, packaging manufacturers, etc. – to commit themselves to using environmentally friendly materials and production processes.

$\mathbf{T}$he paper in this book is made from low- or no-chlorine pulp and is acid free, in conformance with international standards for paper permanency.

Printing: Weihert-Druck GmbH, Darmstadt
Binding: Buchbinderei Schäffer, Grünstadt

Lecture Notes in Computer Science

For information about Vols. 1–587
please contact your bookseller or Springer-Verlag